A HISTORY
OF THE
WHITBY & PICKERING RAILWAY

BY

G. W. J. POTTER.
(The Railway Club.)

2 MAPS AND 40 ILLUSTRATIONS.

SECOND EDITION.

NET PRICE—HALF-A-CROWN

LONDON:
THE LOCOMOTIVE PUBLISHING CO., LTD,
3 AMEN CORNER, E.C.

NEW YORK:
THE DERRY COLLARD CO.,
109 LIBERTY STREET.

1906.

In the interest of creating a more extensive selection of rare historical book reprints, we have chosen to reproduce this title even though it may possibly have occasional imperfections such as missing and blurred pages, missing text, poor pictures, markings, dark backgrounds and other reproduction issues beyond our control. Because this work is culturally important, we have made it available as a part of our commitment to protecting, preserving and promoting the world's literature. Thank you for your understanding.

A

HISTORY

OF THE

WHITBY & PICKERING

RAILWAY.

"FAR FROM THE MADDING CROWD."

FOREWORD.

Seventy years ago a book was published, entitled *Illustrations of the Scenery on the line of the Whitby and Pickering Railway*, which dealt with the railway that had recently been opened between these two Yorkshire towns; it therefore seems an appropriate time to issue this work, which proposes to give, in a popular style, an account of the Whitby & Pickering Railway from its earliest inception down to the present time.

The above mentioned book, which was brought out at the expense of the company with the view of advertising the beautiful scenery of the district, and thus indirectly the railway, was compiled by Mr. Henry Belcher, and was illustrated by 13 fine steel engravings from drawings by George Dodgson. Eight woodcuts also embellished its pages, and the original wood blocks being still in the possession of Messrs. Horne & Son, Whitby, they have very kindly allowed me to have electros made from them, four of which are included in the present work. The steel plates are no longer obtainable, and although half-tone reproductions of the engravings may fail somewhat in suggesting the admirable softness and contrast that is present in the original impressions, little fault, I think, will be found with the four plates herein given. Interest also attaches to them as showing the character of the railway, its accessories, and the artist's conception of the scenery that is met with in close proximity. I have been compelled to quote somewhat freely from contemporary books and pamphlets, and in many cases have simply reproduced the original text instead of paraphrasing it; considering that this was the better way of showing local ideas and sentiment, although a certain amount of disjointedness has perhaps been produced thereby. Few of those who were connected with the line in its early days are now alive, but I have been fortunate enough to meet with some, notably Messrs. Pickering and Wardell, to whom I am indebted for many valuable notes and reminiscences.

My thanks are due to Mr. E. L. Davis, Chief Passenger Agent; Mr. E. M. Horsley, Publicity Department; and Mr. W. Worsdell, Chief Mechanical Engineer; N.E.R., for the trouble that vi.

they have taken in procuring information for me, and in affording facilities for research ; also to other officials of the company who have been, as I have always found them, very courteous and willing to assist in any possible way.

I am fully conscious of the many defects of this little history, but would plead in extenuation that very few sources of information are available, and that I had to make the best of the scanty store, or forego the work altogether. However, as will be seen by these pages, I have chosen the former, thinking that the praiseworthy and successful attempt of the inhabitants of two small towns like Whitby and Pickering to make a railway—when such schemes were to a large extent, untried novelties—deserves to be chronicled.

In conclusion, I cannot do better than quote the following lines from an illuminated MS. of a monk contained in the Library of Corpus Christi College, Cambridge ; merely premising that they have served a somewhat similar purpose once before, and in that case also to a book dealing with Yorkshire.

Mani excilent Notes, though some thinges, waienge the tyme, may be amendid.—Rede, judge,—and thank God for a better light.

G. W. J. P.

South Woodford—June, 1906.

LIST OF ILLUSTRATIONS.

Far from the Madding Crowd		Frontispiece
Fig. 2. Bridge and Tunnel		opp. p. 4
3. Fen Bogs		,, 6
4. South Dale		,, 10
5. Raindale Mill		,, 12
6. Road and Rail Diagram		page 15
7. Old Tunnel		opp. p. 18
8. Old and New Tunnels		,,
9. Weighing Machine House		page 21
10. Bridge at Ruswarp		,, 22
11. Cutting		,, ,,
12. Bridge near Grosmont		,, 23
13. Rail plan		,, 25
14. W. Wardell		opp. p. 30
15. N.E.R. poster		,, 30
16. Kirby		,, 36
17. ,,		,, 36
18. New Tunnel		,, 44
19. Grosmont Station		,, 44
20. Goathland Station		,, 48
21. Sleights Station		,, 48
22. Newton Dale		,, 56
23. Esk Viaduct		,, 56
24. Gradient Diagram		,, 59
25. Map (Autocar routes)		,, 62
26. Engine, No. 272		,, 64
27. ,, ,, 494		,, 64
28. ,, ,, 500		,, 64
29. ,, ,, 1809		,, 64
30. ,, ,, 180		,, 68
31. ,, ,, 472		,, 68
32. ,, ,, 65		,, 68
33. ,, ,, 1033		,, 68
34. ,, ,, 1783		,, 72
35. ,, ,, 1763		,, 72
36. ,, ,, 579		,, 72
37. ,, ,, 2262		,, 72
38. ,, ,, 1667		,, 76
39. ,, ,, 1194		,, 76
40. Bogie Coach		,, 76
41. Relative Diagram		,, 76
42. District Map		,, 80

CHAPTER I.—Early History	page 1
,, II.—Construction and Opening	,, 17
,, III.—1836—1853	,, 35
,, IV.—1854—1905	,, 47
,, V.—Present Day Service	,, 58
,, VI.—Rolling Stock	,, 67
,, VII.—A Journey over the W. & P.R.	,, 77

CHAPTER I.

EARLY HISTORY.

> There is a town, 'twas famed of yore
> For stout-built ships well rigged and stored—
> I mean the port of Whitby.

WHITBY'S position, as a port at the mouth of the River Esk, has from earliest times undoubtedly tended largely to the development of seaborne rather than inland traffic, especially as the town is approached from the interior with difficulty. The first turnpike road leading out of Whitby appears to have been made across the moors in a southerly direction—presumably to Pickering—in 1759. Otherwise the only routes by which one could travel were the bridle ways and the flagged causeways; the often grass-grown remains of the latter being still traceable for many miles in the vicinity of Whitby.

In 1788 communication with York was established by means of a diligence which ran between these towns twice a week; a stage-coach taking its place in 1795. A year later another stage-coach started running between Whitby and Sunderland, and was followed by one to and from Scarboro. On the 15th June, 1814 a new weekly coach was put on between Whitby and Stockton, the route taken being by way of Staithes, Skelton, and Redcar. This was a distance of about 35 miles, and the fares for the complete journey were 14/- for outside passengers, and 20/- for those who preferred to ride in the more comfortable interior. In 1823 a coach, the 'Royal Mail,' ran three times a week from Whitby to York; the stages of the journey being Whitby, Saltersgate, Pickering, Malton, Spital Beck, York.

It is therefore not surprising to find that communication with the inland towns was always in a more or less backward state, especially during the winter months, when travelling over the then bleak and inhospitable moors was extremely uncomfortable and tedious, even if not to say dangerous. The inhabitants seem however to have been fully alive to the necessity of providing other means of transit if it was in any way possible, and as early as 1793 suggestions were made that a canal should be constructed between Whitby and Pickering. A survey of the route intended to be taken was carried out, but after mature consideration the scheme was found impracticable, and was therefore reluctantly abandoned. Matters appear to have then slumbered for some time, but as the highways improved and the coach traffic developed, a means of getting about was provided, even if the travelling by such methods was accomplished under difficulties.

The advantages and future possibilities of railways were evidently appreciated among the wealthier inhabitants of Whitby, and they did not hesitate to financially endorse their opinions; this being, surely, a genuine sort of belief. Thus as far back as 1818, when the Stockton & Darlington Railway Company was laboriously fighting, as a pioneer, the cause of railways in general, against the prejudice and ignorance of many who should have allowed fair play to a scheme, even if they could not concur in all the hopes and aspirations of its promoters, the amount contributed by Whitby people to that project was no inconsiderable sum. In the list of subscribers to the original undertaking of the Stockton & Darlington Railway in 1818—quoted by Mr. Jeans on page 293 of his volume *Jubilee Memorial of the Railway System*—there are no less than 19 names hailing from Whitby, and together contributing a sum of £8,500 out of a total of £120,900, or nearly 14¼ per cent. I look upon this list as extremely creditable to the public spirit of the Whitby people; for although it was to a certain extent, an investment speculation with possibly a good return for their money, still there was a large amount of uncertainty as to how the whole affair would turn out, and it speaks well for them that they were far-sighted enough to believe in the new scheme, and still more to back it with their money.

As Mr. Jeans' volume is now somewhat scarce, and as this list may probably be new to many readers, I have extracted the names of, and amounts subscribed by, all the Whitby people that are so designated and append it herewith.

John Mewburn	100
William Skinner	1000
J. Sanders	1700
J. Sanders for George Sanders	500
Henry Belcher	100
Miss Skinner	200
John Holt	500
Henry Simpson	1000
Richard Kirby	100
Harrison Chiltor	500
William Jameson	500
William Greenside	500
George Langborne	500
Andrew Sanders	300
John Langborne	500
Robert Stevenson, junior	100
Miss Stevenson	100
John Wardell, junior	100
Nathaniel Langborne	200
	£8,500

In 1826, soon after the successful opening of the Stockton & Darlington Railway which took place on the 27th September, 1825, the time for the renewal of the Whitby and Pickering Turnpike Road Act was near at hand, and various projects were afloat for making the roads to Pickering, Scarboro, and Guisboro both shorter and easier; some of the bolder spirits even suggesting the construction of a railway to towns in the interior. Various letters upon the subject were contributed to the *Whitby Repository*, and some pamphlets were published; extracts from the more important are quoted herewith, as they give a fairly comprehensive idea of the trading conditions then prevailing in the old shipbuilding town.

A lengthy epistle from 'Amicus' appeared in the issue for September, 1826, advocating, beside the improvement of the turnpike road between Whitby and Pickering, a railway between these towns. The more salient points of his letter are as follows:

'This proposed alteration [of the road] also favours and may in the end be the means of promoting another plan, which I trust, will at some future time occupy the attention of the town and neighbourhood. It may be thought completely chimerical at present, though I am very sanguine in my ideas and expectations, that it will take place at some time or other; I mean a Railway from Whitby across the moors to the interior of the country, by the way of Pickering: at any rate whether chimerical or not, as your valuable Journal is the medium of conveying information from one to another, I trust your readers will not feel offended at my taking a sort of prospective view of our situation, and the capabilities of improving it. Situated as we are, the only convenient sea-port between the Tees and Humber, and with a rich and fertile country, completely available to us at a distance of only twenty miles; let us not sit down in sullen lethargy, and consider ourselves, and the good town we live in, of so little importance as not to be worth a thought; if we do, we deceive ourselves, and suffer other towns less favourably situated, and possessing not half the advantages we do, to emerge from that insignificance which nature intended them, and by the public spirit of their native sons, rise into an importance they were never designed to possess; nay rival, and even supersede us, by those energies which in us are latent; and which, if aroused and exercised, will prevent their forming even an idea which in competition with us, would be futile and useless . . . . .

'The continental trade, since the peace, has been and is, still likely to be carried on to a very great extent. All the country from Pickering to Scarborough, Malton, Kirby-Moorside, Helmsley, the Dales, &c., is supplied with every article of importation either from Scarborough or Hull, but chiefly from the latter place; whereas if a Railway was made from Whitby to Pickering, all this trade, or nearly so, would fall into our hands; for this natural reason—we could undersell both these places considerably. If there was a Railway from Whitby to Pickering, and from thence to Malton, Baltic produce of every description could be delivered there for nearly 20s. a ton less than it can possibly be from Hull; besides the greater facility in point of time, water carriage being slow and tedious, and liable, for three months in the winter, to be impeded or stopped altogether. The Railway should go in a parallel line with the proposed Turnpike road, and there is not the least doubt, if it could be established, but it would prove a most advantageous speculation. Upwards of 30 years ago a navigable communication between Whitby and Pickering was in agitation; an eminent engineer, Mr. Crosley, was employed to accurately survey, measure, and take the levels on the intermediate ground: the line of the canal was laid down from Whitby, parallel with the river Esk, to Growmond Bridge, from thence by Hunt-house in Gothland to Fensteps, near the present Pickering road at Eller-Beck Bridge, and from thence down Newton Dale to Pickering, making the whole distance about 25 miles; the canal was to have been 4½ feet deep, 30 feet wide at the top, and 18 feet wide at the bottom, such dimensions being sufficient to allow barges of 25 tons burthen to pass each other. The size of each lock was to have been 24 yards long, 4 yards wide, and 4 yards deep, containing 384 cubic yards each.

'The nearest calculation of the time of passing from one place to the other was upwards of eighteen hours, under the most favourable circumstances; but it would, no doubt, have been a much longer time; whereas, by a Railway, which would not be more than nineteen miles, it would not take one-fourth of the time. The expense of the proposed canal was estimated at £66,447; and even at that time when there was a great stagnation of trade. . . . the returns arising from an estimate of the tonnage that was likely to be conveyed thereon . . . . were pronounced, in the report of the committee, at that period, not only to be sufficient to pay the annual sum of £1652 18s. 4d., for agencies, repairs, and other contingent expenses, but to leave also a clear interest of five per cent. to the subscribers. What ought we now to expect to realize from a Railway, which would not cost perhaps half the money, and the annual expense and charges of which would not be one-third of the above sum? To meet the expenses, &c., we possess the advantages which they at that time could not possibly calculate on; the continental trade being now carried on to a great extent. All the Baltic produce, as I have before stated, would be sent to those places from Whitby. All their goods from London would be shipped for Whitby, and transmitted from thence, by the Railway, to their respective purchasers.'

'Amicus' evidently had not the least idea as to how the railway was to get up on to the moors, but this he undoubtedly intended should be done, for he says that the railway is to run

Fig. 2. Bridge and Tunnel at Grosmont as originally built.

parallel with the existing road. Now this involves a rise from about 10 feet above sea-level to an altitude of 945·9 feet, with subsequent dips to 668·9 feet and 564 feet, eventually descending to a level of about 100 feet at Pickering. Of course, these heights are not very extraordinary, but the difficulty lies in the way in which they are approached, most of the ascents being extremely steep. To give an example: at Sleights Bridge adjoining the railway station the datum height is 36·6 feet; at the top of the village, one mile away, it is 323 feet; at the end of another mile, 750 feet; and the summit is attained in about another mile and a quarter. The notorious Blue Bank at the edge of the moor involves a climb of 257 feet in a little over half-a-mile (45 chains), thus giving an average gradient of 1 in 11½. Now as 1 in 100 is reckoned steep for a main line of railway, and few branch lines have anything worse than 1 in 40,—the route from Whitby to Scarboro contains several stretches of this gradient—it will be seen how impossible it would have been to construct a railway along the track suggested by 'Amicus'.

Here it may be advisable to point out to those who have not visited Whitby that the town is surrounded on the landward side by hills in every direction, and that all traffic to and from the interior had to be taken over these natural impediments. By following the course of the Esk a fairly level route might have been obtained, but in many places the construction of a road along its bank would have been all but impracticable. The only place where the old coach-road adheres at all closely to the river is along the level stretch, known as the Carrs, situate between Sleights and Ruswarp; but even here a very steep hill leading out of Ruswarp has to be ascended and another steep one descended before Whitby can be reached.

During the latter half of 1830 Robert Campion, Esq. of Whitby, was making active enquiries for the purpose of establishing a railway from Stockton to Whitby and Pickering. The proposed course to be taken was from the suspension bridge at Stockton by way of Thornaby and Seamer to Stokesley; whence a branch line was to lead to Kirby Moorside or Helmsley. The main route would proceed from Stokesley to Easby and Kildale, thence, parallel with the Esk, by the brow of the Aislaby quarries to Whitby. A line was also projected from Whitby to Pickering with a further extension to Malton.

A survey of the route was determined upon, and at a later date a prospectus of the undertaking with an estimate of the probable expense was to be submitted for public approval.

Canals still numbered many supporters, and in the *Whitby Repository* for January, 1831, the question was asked: 'Would a canal from Whitby to Pickering, for craft of 120 tons burthen, now cost £66,447, as estimated in the year 1794?' This was the canal that was projected in 1793, and referred to in the letter of 'Amicus' quoted above.

At this time Colonel George Cholmley was Lord of the Manor of Whitby, and John Hugill his Liberty Bailiff. In 1830 Hugill published a 70 page pamphlet, in which he addresses the inhabitants of Whitby on the declining state of the town, and the great necessity of improving it; proposes the formation of a company to search for coal in the district; and if successful, to construct a railway from Whitby to Pickering and Malton.

A melancholy picture is drawn of the condition of shipbuilding, formerly the chief industry of the place: many of the shipyards were closed; at others, instead of from 40 to 50 men, only a foreman smith and perhaps half-a-dozen boys were employed; and instead of the 330 men that were engaged in the six shipyards there were scarcely 30 now in work, and these were mostly apprentices.

The whale fishing industry had disappeared, and the local alum works were also closed.

Hugill points out that Liverpool has risen by means of internal navigation and good roads, thus bringing it into close contact with different parts of the kingdom. He suggests that Whitby should proceed in a similar manner to improve its communication with the large towns, and states that a railroad over the moors between Whitby and Pickering may be so contrived as to have less ascent, even in the most hilly parts, than exists in the first mile of the Liverpool & Manchester Railway. This of course refers to the original steep drop of 1 in 48 from Edge Hill to Lime Street where the carriages were hauled up the incline by a stationary engine at the top of the bank. How this desirable end was to be attained Hugill does not state.

A contributor to the *Whitby Repository* of November, 1830, signing himself 'A.B.', reproaches the inhabitants of Whitby for their lack of public spirit, and points out the improvement of internal communication that was then being made in many places by the formation of railways. 'The trade of Whitby,' he says, 'is in the last stage of decline, and owing to the peculiar situation of the town, the speedy construction of a railway communication with the inland country is not only advisable and desirable, but absolutely necessary for the future welfare of the place.'

In the next month's issue 'C.D.' while endorsing the views of 'A.B.', would prefer the railway to run along the valley of the Esk to the neighbourhood of Lealholm Bridge, through Glazedale Swang across the moor to or near Cropton, then to Sinnington and Malton, and connecting by a short branch with Pickering. By this means, the route, though more circuitous, would avoid the fifteen or sixteen miles across a barren moor— out of the way of any cultivated district—that was necessarily encountered by the other line; and by running to Lealholm

Fig. 3. Fen Bogs, entrance to Newton Dale.

Bridge, a distance of ten miles, it would then be in the centre of an agricultural district and within easy reach of many villages. The dues arising from the conveyances of stone, coal from Glazedale, timber, &c., and an almost certain resuscitation of the carriage of farm and dairy produce from the Dales for shipment to the London markets, would, he thinks, prove very advantageous to the shareholders if such a line were constructed.

Next month 'C.D.' estimates that the average quantity of lime brought from Cropton into the different dales from Westerdale to Eskdaleside is 3000 chaldrons; that the cost of conveyance by railway would be considerably less, and that the quantity consumed therefore would probably be doubled. Taking the railway dues as 7s. per chaldron, £2,100 would be earned with probably £900 for coal, a total of £3000 each year. The 25 miles of line to Cropton, he estimated to cost £4,000 per mile, or £100,000 for the entire distance; thus the dues from the transit of the lime and coal would suffice to pay 3% upon the first cost of the railway without taking into account the carriage of merchandise and passengers.

A meeting of the Whitby Literary and Philosophical Society was held at the Museum, on Wednesday, 2nd March, 1831, when Mr. Campion brought forward the report upon the projected railway from Darlington to Whitby, that had been made by Mr. Thomas Storey at Mr. Campion's request.

Mr. Storey had attempted to ascertain which route would benefit that part of the country most, and at the same time offer a probability of the greatest quantity of traffic on a line of railroad between such places; and after examining a very accurate map of Yorkshire, and making the necessary enquiries, the before specified objects appeared to him to be best attained by way of Stokesley and the valley of the river Esk. Accompanied by Mr. T. Mease, of Stokesley, Mr. Storey—who was living at St. Helen's Auckland—took a view of the country lying between the Stockton & Darlington Railway and Whitby. Both being local men it was thought that they would know more of the peculiarities of the district than outsiders.

Two points of junction with the S. & D.R. had been suggested: the first was at the south-east or Yorkshire end of the bridge, then passing on the east side of Thornaby, west side of Stainby Hall and keeping nearly midway between Stainton and Maltby, the course was by the north-east side of Low Field House and Seamer to the south of Tourton; here a branch railroad would take off to Stokesley and terminate at the north end of the town, adjoining the road from Stockton.

The second route left the S. & D.R. at the point where that line crosses the turnpike road from Yarm to Stockton, crossing the Tees by a bridge to be erected for that purpose above Preston Quarry, passing on the north-east side of Barwick, west of Maltby, and joining the first line near Low Field House.

From the point where the branch left the main line the course was near Broughton Mill, south of Easby, crossing the road near the junction of those from Battersby and Kildale, south of Kildale, thence down the valley between Sladhill and Kempswithin, Commondale, and by the Esk to Whitby.

An accurate survey would have to be carried out before any definite decision could be made as to the choice of the best possible route.

The distance from the S. & D.R. to Whitby was about 32 miles by either line, and the length of each of the two proposed sections about 7½ miles.

'On the first portion from the S. & D.R. to Stokesley, an average horse will draw about six tons of goods, independent of carriages, and the same weight on the Whitby line to the foot of the inclined plane at Kildale: twenty tons may be taken up this plane at one time, or more, if thought advisable; one horse would take the latter load from the summit to Whitby, a distance of about 20 miles, and ride in a carriage the whole distance, but would not return with more than half the number of empty carriages.'

So the report reads—presumably the whole of the way from Kildale to Whitby was to be down hill, and Mr. Storey conjectured that the trucks would run all these miles by gravity alone; otherwise the remark as to the horse riding in a carriage is not easily understood.

Taking the dues for coal to be the same as that in force on the S. & D.R., it was calculated that the best household coals might be delivered in Stokesley and Whitby at considerably lower prices than were then obtaining, as will be seen by a perusal of the following table:—

	Present.	Rail-borne.	Saving.
Stokesley Best Coal per ton...	15　0	11　5	3　7
Stokesley Small ditto	10　0	7　11	2　1
Whitby Best ditto	31　8	16　6	15　2
Whitby Small ditto	20　0	13　0	7　0

'Even if the whole of the export duty be taken off the best coal sent coastwise, the advantage in favour of the railroad would still be 10s. 8d. per ton of 20 cwt.

'The quantity of coal necessary to pass over each and every mile of the Stokesley branch, at 1½d. per ton per mile dues for the use thereof, in order to pay 5% yearly interest on the invested capital, and to cover all the expenses of the railroad would be 50,000 tons annually; but the charge on general merchandize being greater than the above rate, and no revenue for coaches having been taken into account, the above quantity will be reduced thereby.

'For the Whitby line, calculating the dues for the use of the road at 1½d. per ton per mile, and 6d. per ton for engine power on the inclined plane, the quantity required would be 60,000 tons annually, independent of the extra charge for merchandize and coaches.'

The report concludes thus:—

'How far it is probable that the before-mentioned quantities will pass along the Railroad annually, I leave with the promoters of the measure to decide; but when I look at the extensive district through which the before-mentioned lines of railway pass, and that connected with it on each side thereof, destitute of fuel to a great extent except peat, requiring lime for its agriculture, producing abundance of valuable freestone for building purposes, basaltic rock for making and repairing roads; alum works partly abandoned on account of the cost of coal at the works, and leading the manufactured article to a place of export; ironstone for the manufacture of iron; and abundance of material for making cement for buildings; and the beautiful opening which will be made up the vale of the Esk into Cleveland, for the supply of grain and produce of that district to good markets, which is at present nearly shut out, from the almost impassable roads therefrom, and which must be a heavy drawback on the value of landed property in that quarter, with various other important advantages the line of communication will afford, I am quite of the opinion, that the speculation will be found advantageous to those who may embark in it, and confer great and lasting benefits on the districts through and adjoining which it passes.'

THOMAS STOREY.

On Friday, 6th May, a meeting was held at the Angel Inn for the purpose of considering the practicability of forming a Railroad from Whitby either to Stockton or Pickering, and the desirableness of raising a fund for defraying the expense of a survey.

R. Campion, Esq. was in the chair.

The meeting was numerously attended; a subscription was entered into to meet the expenses of a survey; and a Committee formed out of the subscribers present, with power to add to their number. Mr. Storey and Mr. Thomas Mewburn, Attorney, of Darlington were both present. Upwards of £200 was raised, which sum was afterwards increased to £410. The survey was to be entered upon as soon as possible, and the cost, it was expected, would be about £500.

In July it is stated that the survey has been commenced, and that Mr. Storey is of opinion that the cost of the line will be several thousands less than he had estimated in his first rough draft—the materials for the work being so near the line and very cheaply procured; also that the traffic from the Dales will be much greater than he had expected.

A pamphlet published at Whitby in December, 1831, by 'A Townsman,' and entitled *Thoughts on a Railway from Whitby into the Interior*, suggested a line to Pickering with a branch to Lealholm Bridge in preference to the Stockton route. The probable return was given as 6 to 7%, and the writer expected that at no distant period the line would be extended to Malton, perhaps to York and Leeds.

The Committee do not appear to have been completely satisfied with Storey's report, and like cautious men of business decided to obtain the opinion of another expert, so in the early summer of 1832 George Stephenson was written to and asked to give his opinion upon the vexed question of route and construction. Hence the following report from the worthy George:

To the Committee of the projected Railway from the port of Whitby.

Gentlemen,
    Having, agreeably with your request, visited the town of Whitby and its neighbourhood, I am now prepared to comply with your instructions—'to report my opinion as to your situation with reference to an improved communication with the interior, and the possibilities of advantage which may be obtained for the town and port of Whitby, and the adjacent country, by means of one or more railways.'

Of the lines of communication which have at different times been projected, two seem more particularly to have engaged the attention of yourselves and the public. One of them consists in the formation of a railway from Whitby up the vale of the river Esk, as far as the Stockton & Darlington Railway, in the vicinity of Yarm; and was proposed with the view of rendering Whitby available as a port for the shipment of the Durham coal. The other project consists in the formation of a railway from Whitby into the interior, in the direction of Pickering; having for one of its principal objects, the supply of that and the adjacent towns of Malton, Kirby, Helmsley, and other neighbouring towns and villages, with a coal very much superior in quality, and of a lower price than that supplied from the southern districts of Yorkshire.

In examining the merits of these two projects, there are three considerations which mainly effect the question of comparative eligibility:—

First, the amount of benefit which, mile for mile, or with a given expenditure, will be derived from the country through which the railway may pass.

Secondly, the extent to which the town of Whitby may be benefitted, or (what is pretty nearly synonymous) the extent to which its fair situation and peculiar advantages as a harbour, may be expected to arise.

Fig. 4. South Dale, near Raindale Inn.

The full investigation of all these points, in addition to an accurate knowledge of both the proposed lines, (which can only be obtained by a detailed survey) requires the possession of the minutest information as to the population of the district, and the amount of its consumption of various commodities, as well as an intimate acquaintance with its agricultural and mineral riches. Such information it will not be expected that I should be in possession of, from my own personal inspection; but from the documents which have been handed to me, and from the general examination which I have made of the districts referred to, I have obtained information, and have been enabled to come to certain general conclusions, which leave no doubt on my mind as to which project will the most certainly and the most extensively, as well as at the least cost, fulfil the conditions above enumerated.

It appears from the survey of the line from Whitby to the Stockton & Darlington Railway, which has been made to Mr. Storey, that the summit of the country, at Kildale, is 651 feet, and of the railway, at the same point, 602 feet above the level of high water mark at Whitby. The power required to raise a given load over this elevation, is equal to that which would be expended in drawing the like load over a distance of upwards of 22 miles of perfectly level ground. On this assumption, therefore, the length of lead from Whitby to the S. & D.R., would be equivalent to a distance of 57 miles of level line; the length of the one surveyed being 35 miles. The question then is shortly this :—

If a railway of such length cannot compete in point of cheapness of transit with the present means of communication, consisting of the railway from Yarm to Middlesboro, (a distance of about 9 miles of very favourable line) and the water communication of vessels thence to Whitby; does the port of Whitby possess advantages over that of Middlesboro to such a degree as to countervail the extra cost of land transit? I should conceive not.

In proceeding to notice the other project, that of a line from Whitby into the interior, in the direction of Pickering, I shall not trouble you with a detailed statement on the subject of probable revenue, because I am satisfied that a statement on this subject, emanating from a Committee of gentlemen, much better qualified, from their local knowledge, to compile such a statement, must be more worthy of public attention, than any calculations of mine would be. I may state, however, that as far as I have investigated this branch of the subject, I have little hesitation in saying, that an estimate of probable revenue, amounting to the sum of £10,500, which has been submitted to me, and which has been prepared I believe with much care, is considerably underrated, insomuch, as many of those articles which I conceive will form leading items of carriage and profit, bear, in the estimate above alluded to, a very small, and in my opinion, a very inadequate proportion to the total amount.

The income arising from the carriage of coal for instance, has only been estimated at £600, whereas, I find with the assistance of the documents that have been laid before me, that the best Durham coal, imported into Whitby, and conveyed thence to Pickering by Railway, may be delivered at the latter place for 2s. or 3s. per ton less price than is at present given for Yorkshire coal of very inferior quality. Looking also to the effect which the execution of the intended Hartlepool Railway and Harbour will have in increasing the facility of supply, and in lowering the price of coal, and considering the great increase which will be occasioned in the demand for coal, for the purpose of lime burning alone ; we shall be justified in calculating upon the consumption of Malton, Pickering, and the adjacent towns (estimated at present I believe at upwards of 43,000 tons) being supplied by the Railway. Assuming the quantity to be 40,000 tons at 1½d. per ton per mile, or 3s. for the whole distance, an income would arise from this source alone of £6,000 per annum.

With reference to the consumption and conveyance of lime, I may observe (what must have struck everyone in passing through this district) that the large tract of land lying between Whitby and Pickering, is now in a most barren and unproductive state, owing merely to the want of lime, which, from passing along the Railway merely as back carriage, would be delivered at a very low rate, and be widely distributed through an extensive tract lying contiguous to the Railway. In order to form some conception of the effect which the great reduction in the price of lime must have, let us suppose the district supplied by the Railway to extend over a distance of 20 miles in length, and over a width of 5 miles, being 2½ miles on each side of the line, these distances would inclose an area of 100 square miles or 64,000 acres, and as the whole of this tract requires liming, and as each acre should have (on a very moderate computation) 6 tons every four years or 1½ tons per annum, the annual consumption of lime would amount to 96,000 tons, and supposing the average distance over which this quantity taken, to be 12 miles at 1½d. per ton per mile, including tonnage rate and haulage ; the carriage of this article would annually yield to the Railway company the sum of £7,200 and the benefit that must accrue to the landholders is incalculable. Amongst other articles the use of which will be greatly extended by the provision of a cheap means of transit, I may instance whinstone ; a material which will make an invaluable substitute for the perishable stone with which the roads in this part of Yorkshire, and as far as York, are at present repaired. Nor will the demand for it, I conceive, be confined to the district lying within the distance of 20 or 30 miles, for we find that a similar description of stone is at present conveyed from

FIG. 5. RAINDALE MILL.

Leicestershire to London by land over a distance of upwards of 100 miles. It is not therefore unreasonable to suppose that the whinstone of Egton Bridge and Goathland, lying within 6 or 7 miles of one of the finest harbours in England, and conveyed to that harbour by a descending Railway, may be delivered in London at a much less price than is at present paid. Coal, lime, and whinstone, though they have been specially noticed, are by no means the only—probably not the principal—articles, an increased consumption of which will be the consequence of diminished cost, and additional facilities of transit. I might enumerate freestone from Eskdale to Whitby. Oak and Ash timber from Pickering to Whitby. Baltic and American timber from Whitby to Pickering. Groceries, drugs, fish, &c., from Whitby to Pickering and the interior generally. Agricultural produce from the interior to Whitby. The speed and cheapness of Railway communication must likewise induce an increased amount of travelling, which, whilst tending to promote mercantile activity, will, I have no doubt, contribute largely to the income of the company.

The cursory examination of the country which my late visit allowed me, will not enable me to enter into a detailed description of the line, of which, I would recommend an accurate survey to be made, and which alone will enable me to give any satisfactory description of its merits. I may say, however, that I am not aware of the occurrence of any formidable obstacle on any part of the line, which, by a judicious selection of the ground, may not be avoided. I will now briefly describe the general course of the line;—it would proceed from Whitby, as far as Growmond, up the vale of the Esk, the crossing of which river may be rendered less frequent by diverting its course in some instances where the line intersects it. At Growmond the line would pass into the Goathland Valley, the rise of which for about one mile in length is abrupt; but with the exception of this short distance, the whole of the line up Goathland, and thence through Newton-Dale to Pickering, appears to be very favourable; and should the detailed survey bear out my present impressions of the nature of the country, I think, a line of Railway may be laid for £2,000 per mile, which, for 24 miles, the supposed distance between Whitby and Pickering, would amount to £48,000.

This mileage estimate, I should observe, is founded on the supposition that the landowners, the value of whose property will be so greatly enhanced by the execution of the proposed Railway, will give all the land that is required.

The whole of the work should be substantially executed, but be of the very plainest description. As soon as the main line is completed, there is no doubt that the Company will find it their interest to lay down several short branches into the rich mineral districts adjoining the line, and that these branches will prove valuable feeders to the main line. I have thought it better, however, for the present, to abstain from adverting to them more particularly.

In conclusion, I will merely remark, that, after taking a general review of the merits of this scheme, it appears to me to be deserving of the most cordial support of all parties; of the inhabitants of Whitby, from its insuring both to the town and harbour an increased activity of trade :—of the landowners, from its affording them the opportunity of converting an immense barren tract into fertile land :—of the inhabitants of Pickering, and all the towns and villages of the Northern District of Yorkshire, from its enabling them to obtain coal (far superior to that with which they are at present supplied) as well as other commodities imported into Whitby, at a considerably lower price: and, lastly, if the public and the capitalists, from the prospect (amounting, I conceive, to certainty) that the revenue arising from the use of the Whitby & Pickering Railway, will amply remunerate the proprietors for the money invested.

I have the honour to be, gentlemen,
Your most obedient servant,
GEORGE STEPHENSON.

July 5th, 1832.

P.S. Thinking it would be satisfactory to the Committee to know of what items the sum of £2,000, which I have estimated as the probable cost per mile, is composed, I have thought it best to append the statement given below.

Probable amount required for the completion of one mile of the Whitby Railway.

	£	s.	d.
Rails, weighing 40lbs. per yard, 63 tons per mile of single Railway, which at £9 per ton	567	0	0
Chairs, weighing 12lbs. each, say 20 tons per mile, at £6 16s. per ton	130	0	0
Keys and Pins, ½lb. each, 2 tons 12 cwt. per mile, at £20 per ton	50	0	0
Oak Plugs, 7½ thousand per mile at £1 per thousand	7	10	0
Blocks, at 1s. each, 3520 per mile	176	0	0
Fencing, at 2s. per lineal yard, £176 per mile; but as Fencing is supposed to be put down, along only half the distance, the average cost per mile may be taken at	88	0	0
Laying the rails and ballasting the way, at 2s. 6d. per lineal yard	220	0	0

PICKERING RAILWAY.

	£	s.	d.
Earthwork, say	300	0	0
Bridges and Culverts, say	100	0	0
Add for sidings	150	0	0
Contingencies...	211	10	0
Assumed total cost per mile	£2000	0	0

From an indirect source it has been found possible to reproduce herewith what is probably a part of the gradient diagram (Fig. 6.) that accompanied the prospectus, and which showed the relative heights and inclinations of the road and the projected railway. This is taken from *Descriptions, Geological, Antiquarian, and Topographical, of East Yorkshire*, published in 1855, and written by Robert Knox of Scarborough; and the author's remarks relative thereto are extremely curious.

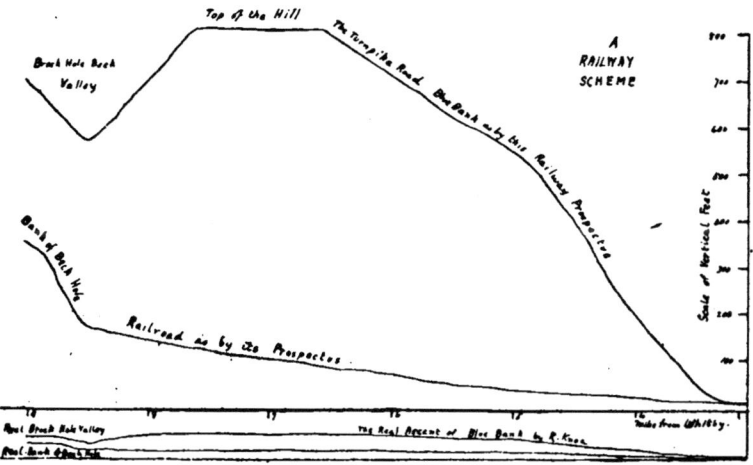

FIG. 6 ROAD AND RAILWAY DIAGRAM.

'The plate exhibits the engineer's comparative sections of the hills over which the high road, and this railroad, pass for some distance southward from Esk Dale; and the sections which I have drawn of the same ascents. Tyroes will, doubtless, be astonished on beholding the difference of the upper diagram, and mine beneath, representing the true elevations of the very same inclines. Did the projector of that plan, drawn upon false principles, suppose the calculating people of Whitby would comprehend a comparative truth squeezed out from between two fictions, better than from the plain truth itself? The cost of this railroad was about £120,000, and it was sold, in 1844, to the Midland Railway Company for £83,000.'

Knox, judging from his book, was undoubtedly a man of great importance in his own estimation; his opinions, and his only, were always right. As the gradient diagram was another person's work, it is not surprising to find that he prefers the true elevations—which in many cases would not show a perceptible difference—to the more usual method of indicating the changes of gradient on a larger scale, in this case about the ratio of 18 or 19 to 1—thus graphically showing the rise and fall in an unmistakable manner. Nevertheless, in the large map accompanying his book, he does not hesitate to draw his sections in a similar manner: 'nearly four times too high' as he innocently remarks. His accuracy is shown in the last sentence of his account of the railway: the fact being that the railway was sold legally in 1845, though arrangements would probably be concluded in 1844; that the purchasers were the York & North Midland Railway, a totally different company;—and that the price agreed upon was £80,000.

Brock Hole Beck is now usually called Brocka Beck.

A meeting was held at the Angel Inn, Whitby, on Wednesday, 12th September, 1832, at which Stephenson's report was brought forward by the sub-committee. Its reading gave great satisfaction to the gentlemen present, and all seemed to be quite assured that the formation of this line would not only be profitable to the shareholders, but highly beneficial to the towns at each extremity, as well as to the country through which it would pass. The estimated cost was put at under £80,000, and it was calculated from authentic data, that the traffic which might be fairly expected on the line, would pay a nett return of 10% to the shareholders. At the conclusion of the meeting, a share list was opened, and nearly £30,000 was subscribed on the spot.

Here it may be remarked that Whitby was, largely through the exertion of Mr. Richard Moorsom, created a borough in 1832. However, Mr. Moorson was not allowed a walk-over, as Mr. Aaron Chapman, who was in favour of the making of the railway, was brought forward in the Conservative interest, and the latter was duly elected at the poll held in December 1832.

Although the route preferred by Mr. Campion had not been adopted, this zealous promoter of a railway from Whitby did not hesitate to give his support to the Pickering line; saying 'He thought that it was better to have a railway in that direction rather than not to have one at all.'

Doubtless opinion was somewhat divided in the town as to which was the better route to adopt, and there would sure to be some who were dubious as to the ultimate profit of the undertaking; but minor differences seem to have been waived, and eventually it was decided to make a speedy application to Parliament for the necessary powers to construct a railway from Whitby to Pickering.

CHAPTER II.

CONSTRUCTION AND OPENING.

> Along the river's winding shore,
> Or o'er its pebbly strand,
> A road appears unknown of yore,
> By modern science planned.
>
> And as up Eskdale's ample range
> It skirts each wood and dene,
> More grand, more varied is each change,
> More lovely grows the scene.

THE exertions of the promoters were duly rewarded with success, for on 6th May, 1833 their Bill received the Royal Assent. The Act (3 William IV. cap. XXXV.) contained 177 sections, and it will be interesting to quote—largely diverted of their legal phraseology—some of the more important.

Eight hundred shares of £100 each, and borrowing powers to the extent of £25,000 was the financial limit allowed to the company by the Act.

No buildings were to be erected on the property of Edmund Turton, the then owner of Larpool Hall.

Power was given to divert the River Esk, also the Goadland and Pickering Becks where necessary.

The works were not to deviate more than 100 yards from the plan. The land taken for the railway was not to exceed 22 yards in breadth, except where a greater breadth was required for carriages to wait, load or unload, turn or pass each other, or for embankments and cuttings; and then not in any place to exceed 150 yards except at the Whitby and Pickering termini. An additional 15 acres was allowed for the stations, &c.

The gauge or distance between the rails was not to be less than 4 feet 8 inches and the distance between the outside edges of the rails was not to exceed 5 feet 1 inch.

Section 55 is interesting as provision is therein made as to the employment of the Outram type of rails should such be used. The Outram plate-way was invented by Mr. Benjamin Outram and his father, and was first used at Sheffield in 1776. It consisted of cast-iron plates, one yard in length, having a ledge or flange upon the inner side to keep the wheels upon the track, and which were spiked down to stone blocks. A few years later, in 1789, Mr. William Jessop invented the edge-railway, in which the flange was transferred from the plates to the wheels. The lines that used this system were for a considerable time described as edge-railways to distinguish them from the plate-ways of Outram. The men employed to fix the plates or rails to the stone blocks or wooden sleepers were known respectively as plate-layers and rail-layers; curiously enough the former term has survived to the present day, but no one ever speaks of a rail-layer now. This is a pity, as it is the correct word, and to call a rail-layer a plate-layer is both misleading and inaccurate.

The section referred to reads as follows:—

> When the said Railway shall cross any Public Highway the Ledge or Flanch of such Railway for the purpose of guiding the Wheels of the Carriages thereupon shall not rise above nor sink below the Level of such Road more than One Inch.

However the Outram system was not adopted, the line being laid with fish-bellied rails fastened to stone blocks.

Bridges over the railway were required to have an arch of not less than 15 feet in width, with its centre 16 feet high; and the gradient of the road leading to and passing over it was not to exceed 1 in 13. This was another instance of careful precaution, as upon the whole of the original route there was no bridge whatever over the line, and only one tunnel. Such bridges as were under the railway were built for crossing the river, and all but one of the roads were crossed on the level.

The first General Meeting was to be held within six calendar months after the passing of the Act. The succeeding Annual General Meetings were to be held on the first Tuesday in May, or within 14 days from that time, at Whitby.

Section 76 states that 18 persons are to be the first Directors, 12 to reside within 7 miles of Whitby or Pickering. Their qualification was to be 5 shares, and 5 could form a quorum. Their names as given in the Act are—

Joseph Barker, Barker William Barker, John Barry, Robert Barry, Charles Belcher, William Benson, Robert Campion, John Campion, Abel Chapman, Edward Chapman, Aaron Chapman, John Chapman, William Chapman, George Cholmley, Thomas Fishburn, John Frankland, Nicholas King, John Langborne, Richard Moorsom, Richard Ripley, Thomas Simpson, Henry Simpson, William Henry Smith, Gideon Smales, John Watson, James Wilkinson.

Negative by] [*G. W. J. Potter.*
FIG. 7. THE OLD HORSE RAILWAY TUNNEL, GROSMONT.

FIG. 8. OLD AND NEW TUNNELS, GROSMONT.

All the early railways were regarded as a type of public road or highway; and generally speaking, provided that the tolls were paid and proper vehicles used, anyone was at liberty to bring his own carriages or trucks upon the line; the company usually providing the requisite motive power. To a certain extent this practice prevails to-day, more especially with regard to mineral traffic, which is largely conveyed in trucks belonging to the colliery owners. The section referring to this practice is No. 110 and reads thus:—

> That all Persons shall have free liberty to pass along and to use and employ the said Railway with Carriages properly constructed as by this Act directed, upon Payment only of such Rates and Tolls as shall be demanded by the said Company.

The maximum tolls authorised were 2d. per ton per mile for carriage of materials for repair of roads; 3d. for coal, lime, iron, bricks, potatoes, kelp; 4d. for corn, flour, coke, manufactured iron, steel, timber, hay; 5d. for malt, meat, groceries, wool, fruit, vegetables; and a 6d. rate for all things not before particularised. The rate for passengers was 2d. per mile. Carriages weighing not more than two tons were conveyed on trucks and charged 9d. per mile.

For any distance less than 5 miles travelled on the railway, the company were empowered to charge as for 5 miles, but it does not appear that this was ever carried out.

An extra charge of 1s. per ton was made for all goods taken up the incline, but this did not apply to those coming down the bank.

The limit of weight imposed on all vehicles running on the line was 4 tons, or 8 tons when loaded.

Section 114 states that

> It shall be lawful for the said Company and they are hereby empowered to provide locomotive Engines or other Power for the drawing or propelling of any Articles, Matters, &c. upon the said Railway.

But a little later on, namely in Section 134, it is distinctly stated that

> It shall not be lawful for the said Company, or for any other Corporation or Person whatsoever, to use or employ locomotive Steam Engines upon the said Railway.

Presumably this apparent contradiction was considered necessary—of course it would be by the lawyers, clerks, etc., as it all meant more money for them to be taken out of the pockets of the shareholders—also the sections as to Outram-rails, over-bridges, already referred to, but what a striking commentary on the practices of English law. First grant permission for a certain thing, and then a few pages later absolutely annul the permission. No wonder that all persons are advised not to go to law, for undoubtedly the chief benefit is obtained by the lawyers, and that very often in a not particularly creditable manner. A somewhat similar instance occurs in a later Act: here section 33 allows the company to charge as for 5 miles any journey taken that is under that distance (as in the 1st Act); section 34 raises the distance and charge to 6 miles, and of course with a copious amount of verbiage. What need is there for the two sections, and why would not a simple statement of facts answer all purposes?

A few days after the passing of the Bill—namely, on 25th May—one William Thompson, of whom we shall hear later, published a 16-page pamphlet entitled *The Whitby & Pickering Railway; its probable traffic and revenue.*

It evidently met with a good reception in the neighbourhood as a second edition was brought out, dated 11th June; both are now very scarce and copies are but rarely met with. The work dealt chiefly with the carriage of coals, lime, timber, whinstone, flagstone and freestone; and after careful consideration put the dues that would be earned by the haulage of this traffic as follows:

	Tons.	£	s.	d.
Coal	22,000	3850	0	0
Lime and Limestone	15,000	1687	10	0
Timber	3,000	1200	0	0
Whinstone	8,000	1050	0	0
Flag and Freestone	—	1000	0	0
		8787	10	0

Allowing nearly £3,000 for working expenses of the line, &c., the writer concluded that the net sum available would be £6,000 or sufficient to pay 7½% to the shareholders for the carriage of these items only.

Thompson's statements were controverted by 'A Looker-on,' hailing from Pickering, in *The Whitby and Pickering Railway: An impartial examination of the estimates published relative to that undertaking.* Malton, 1834; and an annual deficiency of at least £175 was prophesied even under the most favourable circumstances.

The Directors soon set to work with a will, and by August the contract for the construction of the first section—Boghall to Sleights—had been let, and that upon very favourable terms. The actual making of the line may be said to have commenced on the 10th September, 1833, when its indefatigable promoter, Robert Campion, had the privilege and pleasure of turning the first spadeful of earth that day near Boghall. The railway began at a point that was originally occupied by the ship-building yard of Messrs. Fishburn and Brodrick, this being situated on the west side of the harbour, and somewhat to the south of the present station. The course of the Esk was then followed in a southerly direction; but the banks of the river here sloping very steeply, a wall had to be built, and the line was carried along it past the quay and warehouse of the Whitby Stone Company. The Weighing Machine House was situated close by; a view of it in its original condition is herewith appended, and it may be noted that the somewhat dilapidated remains of the building are still to be seen on the river side of the line.

FIG. 9. WEIGHING MACHINE HOUSE.

After a sharp curve to the west had been made, the first difficult task was encountered: the diversion of the Esk. The river here made a long loop, and the mere bridging of it would not suffice, as being tidal up to and beyond this point, ships would require to come up, thus necessitating two swing-bridges with their attendant drawbacks and certain delay to the traffic. It was therefore decided that the more satisfactory plan would be to do away with this loop by cutting it off and making a new channel for the river; thus avoiding the expense of bridge-building and enabling the line to be kept to the north side of the river until Ruswarp was reached. The portion cut off remained for some years as a small lake, and it was a favourite resort of eel-fishers, and in winter of skaters; but it gradually drained away, and little now remains to show that the river once flowed there. The pedestrian from Whitby to Ruswarp, by way of the fields, practically follows from Fitz Steps the bend of the river's original course; and where the Foundry now stands, a bone-crushing and saw mill was erected shortly after the opening of the line.

At Ruswarp, the first and longest bridge had to be erected. It was constructed of Baltic fir. and carried across the river in a diagonal direction. It was 312 feet in length, divided into five portions of 62 feet span each; and the framework of the whole was supported upon four rows of piles fourteen inches square—placed obliquely so as to offer the least possible resistance to the natural and tidal currents of the river—and firmly strapped together by iron bands. The expense of this bridge, including the masonry, extras, and cornices, was £1575. A view of the original bridge is now given.

FIG. 10. BRIDGE AT RUSWARP.

Near here a suspension bridge across the river for foot passengers had been erected by James Wilson, Esq., M.P. in 1825, which was eventually washed away in a heavy storm.

The next two miles gave much trouble to the contractors as a considerable amount of boggy ground was met with, numerous springs were encountered, and the banks and cuttings showed a tendency to give way. After passing Sleights Bridge, and curving round Esk Hall, the line then ran upon an embankment for about a mile in a nearly direct line, crossing the river twice; and immediately after the latter bridge passing the ruins of Eskdale chapel. Some cuttings at a little distance further along had to be made through the alum rock, and the working of these proved tedious owing to the hardness of the schistus. One of these cuttings is illustrated by the following block.

FIG. 11. CUTTING IN ESKDALE.

In the comparatively short distance between Sleights Bridge and the Tunnel Inn, Grosmont—about 3½ miles—no less than 8 bridges were constructed. Some were built across the loops of the Esk to avoid lengthy detours, and others were rendered necessary by the extreme steepness of the banks and that alternately on one side and the other. At one point the railway had to be supported by a high and massive wall of masonry, skirting the side of the precipitous bank for a considerable distance. The eighth bridge over the Esk is represented in the following woodcut; this and another having been crossed, the site of Grosmont Priory was next passed, and the Tunnel Inn reached.

FIG. 12. BRIDGE NEAR GROSMONT.

Hence the route lay forward through the Vale of Goathland, and this could only be entered by means of a tunnel. Fig. 2 is reproduced from one of the original steel engravings and gives a capital idea of the beautiful and well-wooded country, together with the bridge over the Murk Esk and the tunnel with its quaint castellated front. Fortunately the ridge to be pierced was not of great width, and the tunnel was only required to be 130 yards in length. The side walls were vertical for 9 feet, and supported an 18-inch arch of brickwork. The width was 10 feet, and the height 14 feet to the soffite of the roof. It was constructed of stone obtained from the local quarries of Leaserigg hard by.

Fig. 8 shows the old and the new tunnels: the length of the latter being 143 yards, width about 24 feet, and height about 21 feet.

From the tunnel the line continued to gradually rise, passing in about a mile the Quarries of the Whitby Stone Company which were situated on the brow of the hill to the west of the railway. It was then carried through the great Whinstone dyke which extends in a succession of straight lines from Middleton in Teesdale to Staintondale near Scarboro. The dyke is generally from 40 to 60 feet in breadth, and many cases rises to the surface of the ground, but in other parts is concealed by the alluvial formations. Considerable quantities of scoriae and iron slag were met with near here, showing most decidedly that the rich veins of iron ore found in the vicinity were not only known, but also wrought, at a period far beyond the date of any tradition on the subject.

Some 8½ miles from Whitby, a romantic spot called Beck Hole was reached; deriving its name from the meeting of two moorland becks or streams: the Ellerbeck which comes from the southeast, and the Wheeldale beck from the west. At this point an inclination of more than 200 feet above sea level was attained, and here was situated the foot of the inclined plane, that was constructed hence to Goathland, and about which so much was destined to be heard during the coming years. The route was cut through a wood, and thus had the appearance of a fine curved avenue of nearly a mile in length; the upper part opening out upon the village green of Goathland. The average rate of ascent was 1 in 15, although the steepest portion was 1 in 10·89; the total length being about 1500 yards.

A somewhat novel method of working the incline was introduced, for as descending loads of wagons or carriages more than sufficient to balance the weight of those to be hauled up could not always be depended upon, additional help was necessary, and this was provided in the shape of tanks mounted on railway wheels and filled with water, of which a plentiful supply was always available and easily obtained. Arrived at the bottom the water was allowed to run away, and the empty tanks were drawn up again for future service.

The rope wheel which was fixed in a horizontal position at the top of the incline was of 10 feet diameter and 5 inches in depth; and was made with a rim of hollow section to receive the 4½ inch rope. The latter ran on sheaves, 10 inches in diameter, set in iron frames which were let into stone blocks; there being 174 of these sheaves placed at intervals of 8 yards all along the incline. As the track was considerably curved in parts, the sheaves were at those places fixed at different degrees of inclination, and wooden friction rollers of 2 feet in length and 6 inches in diameter were also provided to afford the rope sufficient play where necessary.

In 1836 the time taken to haul a coach up the incline by this method was usually about 4½ minutes. A few years later this plan was abandoned, and a steam winding engine was placed at the Goathland end of the bank.

About 2½ miles from the incline top, and at an equal distance from each terminus, the summit level of the line was attained at a point known as Fen Bogs, a huge morass situated between lofty cliffs.

Fig. 3 shews the entrance to Newton Dale, Fen Bogs filling the central portion of the picture. This spot is the source whence springs the Pickering Beck and which is a constant companion of the railway to Pickering. Soon after passing that town it unites with the Derwent, which falls into the Humber, and thus its waters eventually join the sea after a course of nearly 100 miles; though rising out of a hill which commands an extensive view of the North Sea at only a few miles distance.

Much difficulty was encountered in making a solid road over the bog, immense quantities of material being swallowed up by it; and like Chat Moss, on the Liverpool and Manchester line, it was eventually conquered by the gradual sinking of hurdles covered with cut moss, heather, young trees, &c. thus slowly driving out the water and yet retaining a foundation.

Hence the way laid, by many sharp curves and turns, through the high cliffs on each hand, along the course of a narrow moorland stream, while others gushed down from the hills. At times all further progress seemed arrested by the projecting cliffs and eminences that apparently closed in the valley completely. A sharp bend around the foot of the hill, and another vista of woodland opened out to the traveller, the scenery gradually becoming less wild, until near Pickering it assumed the aspect of a beatiful park-like yet well-wooded country.

A few words may now be said upon the permanent way, &c., of the original undertaking, the particulars being chiefly derived from the pages of Messrs. Belcher and Whishaw.

The gauge, or distance between the rails, was that always adopted by Stephenson, 4 feet 8½ inches, and which is now practically the standard gauge of the world.

The rails were of the fishbellied type and 15 feet in length, weighing 40lbs. to the yard—thus Belcher, Whishaw says 35lbs. The joints were in some cases scarfed, and in others half-lapped, these latter being considered the best. The annexed sketch, which however is not drawn to scale, should make the difference between the two systems easily understood without further description.

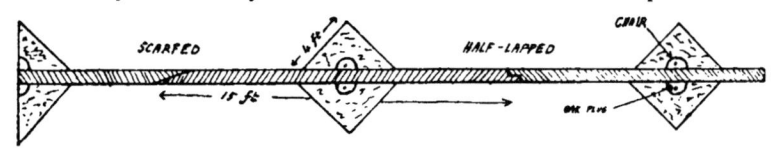

Plan of RAIL-JOINTS, CHAIRS, and STONE BLOCKS.

The chairs weighed from 14lb. to 16lb. each, and were fixed to stone blocks of 4 feet cube, these being placed diagonally. At the outset it is probable that the blocks were used throughout except on the bridges, but later on their employment appears to have been confined to the cuttings; transverse wooden sleepers being used on the embankments. Upon the bridges the chairs were bolted down to the wooden planking of the floor.

Many of the curves were of very short radius, several being of about 20 chains, while the most severe had only a radius of 10 and 12 chains.

The entire distance of the railway was 23·962 miles, and from Whitby to the summit level was 11¾ miles, where a height was attained of 520 feet, implying a rise of 515 feet from the commencement of the line at Whitby; thence to Pickering the fall was about 434 feet. With the exception of a very short piece at the beginning of the line which descended at the rate of 1 in 808, the whole route from Whitby to the summit was uphill; the eleven gradients encountered varying from 1 in 74 to 1 in 1691. The two steepest, 1 in 10·89 and 28·38, situated between Beck Hole and Goathland, were worked by machinery. At the summit was a level plane of 20¾ chains, and from that point all was downhill to Pickering; the steepest slopes being 44·5, 55, 58·38, 68, and the remainder of the 13 planes at lesser inclinations. The last 3½ miles into Pickering were at 1 in 1056, and this gentle fall may almost be considered as equivalent to a level.

By the early part of 1835 the construction of the line had advanced far enough to warrant the working of a temporary service over a portion of the route, so on the 8th of June a coach ran an inaugural trip from Whitby to the Tunnel Inn and back; this service being continued during the summer months. During the first three months of its running, the large number of 6,000 persons travelled to and fro, attracted doubtless by the novelty of the conveyance, and the ease with which the beautiful scenery could be easily enjoyed. At a later date a coach also ran locally between Pickering and Raindale, thus allowing the residents in the two chief towns an opportunity of becoming acquainted with the new method of travelling.

Thursday, the 26th of May 1836, was fixed as the day for the official opening of the line throughout, and when the morning broke forth most brilliantly—many know how brilliant and beautiful it can be at Whitby, especially in the early summer—and with every prospect of its continuance during the day, all the inhabitants and visitors were naturally in high spirits. The bells of the old parish church rang merry peals, and by half-past seven crowds of people began to gather at the Angel Inn, where the band had assembled. Soon afterwards the procession was here formed and then made its way to the station in the following order: four constables; some of the railway workmen; Mr. Wilkinson, chief police officer; the Whitby Brass Band; Robert Campion, Esq., chairman; Thomas Fishburn, Esq., deputy chairman; the directors; the engineers and solicitors; flags; gentlemen three abreast; the remainder of the workmen and constables.

Tickets for places in the carriages had been issued to all such of the proprietors as applied for them not later than the 19th of May; thus the number of those intending to be present was known and the requisite number of carriages provided, together with an additional vehicle for the accommodation of strangers who might be visiting the old town on that date. Barriers protected the approaches to the offices, and placards indicated the doors through which the first and second class passengers were to enter and exchange their invitations for tickets; these had to be shown to the guard upon commencing the journey, and delivered to the same personage when the return was made from Pickering. As the location of each seat was indicated on the ticket, each person knew where he had to sit and had the assurance that his place was reserved for him.

The time for departure had been fixed for 8.0 a.m., and the merry party was expected to arrive at Pickering soon after 11.0 a.m.

The ladies had taken their seats previously to the arrival of the procession, and the passengers all being seated a bell was rung; the horses were then brought out and attached to the carriages. Each coachman and guard had a green card placed in his hat showing the coach to which they belonged. Upon the bell again ringing, the coaches started off at a brisk pace amid much cheering from the assembled crowds. The speed of the various coaches was regulated by the display of different coloured flags entrusted to the guards—the whole being under the control of Messrs. Swanwick and Harding. A white flag meant 'go on'; a red 'go slow'; and a blue 'stop.' This usage of flags for signalling purposes was in the early days of railway life fairly common, but it has been largely supplanted by the improved methods of modern signalling, and beyond the starting flags of the guards but little employment of this system can be found now-a-days in England.

Arrived at the Tunnel Inn (now Grosmont) the lime kilns then being built for the Whitby and Grosmont Lime Company were pointed out to the party; likewise at Leaserigg, the operation of sending a wagon-load of stone from the quarries of the Whitby Stone Company down the steep face of the cliff by a self-acting inclined plane. Both these companies had with others been brought into being by the opening of the line.

The next stoppage was at the foot of the inclined plane at Beck Hole where the horses were detached; here the passengers had an excellent opportunity of inspecting this unknown place about which so much had been heard, for as usual, the drawbacks of its plan and working had been greatly exaggerated by those who were not favourable to the undertaking. Many, of course, had not seen the place before, and were agreeably surprised to find how smoothly everything went; for on the signal being given, three of the carriages with their load of passengers glided up the steep ascent with a pleasing, easy, and rapid pace, and the journey over this section was pronounced to be quite as pleasant as upon any other part of the route. The other carriages followed in similar groups, the band during the time playing various pieces of music to the delight of the country people, who had collected in large numbers at the top of the inclined plane, and who with waving of colours and firing of guns heartily welcomed the visitors.

The journey was then resumed to a spot where the line falls rather rapidly; this point would be about 15 miles from Whitby, where the present-day gradients are 1 in 50, 86, 58, 86, this continuing for a little over two miles, and gradually easing off through Levisham station. At the top of this slope the horses were again unyoked and the coaches connected together with coupling-bars; the train then started off, soon reaching a rapid pace, and in order to gratify the company, a speed of 30 miles per hour was allowed to be obtained; this of course gradually lessened after the steepest portions had been passed, but a rate of 14 or 15 miles an hour was kept up for some time; much amusement being caused by the sight of several gentlemen on horseback racing away after each other to overtake and beat the carriages into Pickering. I cannot do better than here insert an account of the opening as seen from the point of view of a Pickering man.

'About nine in the morning the church bells of Pickering began to announce the opening of the new railroad, and people began to draw near to the place where the carriages had to pass. Five bands of music were stationed in proper places for the best effect. About ten, several pieces of cannon were planted opposite the Castle, which were fired at intervals. About eleven the hills on each side of the railroad were covered with people of the first rank, and great anxiety was evinced for the appearance of the train of carriages. At a quarter past twelve the cannon announced the train in sight; all the bands struck up and played suitable pieces. We never experienced so fine a sight when the carriages came up; the first was filled with ladies and gentlemen from Whitby, and every carriage had banners with the design of the railway neatly executed.'

The late arrival was caused by the bad behaviour of *Lady Hilda*, a new carriage that was being tried for the first time that day, and which signalised the event by running off the line three times soon after commencing the journey. After the third derailment the passengers were transferred to another vehicle, and the *Lady Hilda* was left behind.

A breakfast had been prepared at the Black Swan Inn, so the procession was quickly formed, and with the Pickering band leading, passed up the town to that famous hostelry. Nearly 300 persons partook of the repast, the cost being, so it is chronicled, 2/6 per head.

The train of carriages left Pickering at 2.15 p.m. on the return journey.

Upon arriving at the inclined plane between Goathland and Beck Hole, to show the passengers the command that the officials possessed over the descent of the carriages, the brakes were applied when the coaches were going down the slope, and the train gradually brought to a standstill: the rope was then disengaged, the brakes released, and the occupants of the coaches were gratified in travelling at about 20 miles an hour down the incline and for some distance over the level ground at the foot of the bank. The horses were once more brought into action, and took the carriages in fine style into Whitby, arriving there almost exactly at the time appointed, namely 5.0 p.m.

The festive proceedings were continued by a dinner at the Angel Hotel, to which some 70 guests sat down. Toasts and speeches followed, the party eventually breaking up at 2.0 a.m.

The Whitby & Pickering Railway was now an accomplished fact, and it may be of interest to give a short account of the vehicles that were used in the early days of its history; such notes as are here presented being largely derived from the pages of Whishaw, an early and prominent writer on the technical details of railway life.

The carriages appear to have been of two kinds, open and closed; the latter weighing about $2\tfrac{3}{4}$ tons. They ran upon four wheels which were of 3 feet diameter. The cost of each vehicle was £100 for the open, and £280 for the closed types. Each carriage was drawn by one horse—a similar practice obtaining upon the Edinburgh & Dalkeith Railway and other lines about that time—the driver sitting in a dickey placed at the front with a footboard beneath, something after the style of a modern omnibus. A lever to apply the brake to the wheels was placed within convenient reach of the driver.

The wagon bodies were constructed of wood with bottoms of sheet iron, the sides being of $1\tfrac{1}{8}$ inch deal, and were so made that either end could be removed for the purpose of loading and unloading the freight. The top length of the wagon was 8 ft. 5 ins., and the bottom 7 ft. 9 ins.; the width 6 ft. 2 ins.; and height above the soles 2 ft. 6 ins. The soles were 10 inches in depth and projected 13 inches at each end. The wagons were mounted on wheels of the same diameter as that employed for the passenger carriages, namely, 3 feet, and were fitted with springs; the net weight being $34\tfrac{1}{4}$ cwt. Trucks were also provided, these were somewhat lighter, as their weight is given as $28\tfrac{3}{4}$ cwt.

So much for the technical details: fortunately some interesting notes on the working of the coaches can now be added, these having been told to the writer by William Wardell, who was employed as a postillion-rider by the company. In the early days two coaches made the sum total of the passenger rolling stock; these were the *Lady Hilda* and the *Premier*, both painted yellow; at a later date another was added, *Transit*, this being painted green. Practically the vehicles were a transference of the ordinary stage coach body to a railway truck, with of course the necessary adaptations to fit it for its new work. In tracing the growth and development of English railway life, it will be found that all the ideas and practices of the railway were modelled on stage-coach traditions, these being modified or superseded as they were found by practice to be inconvenient.

The seating accommodation on these coaches was not rigidly defined: thus six sat inside, four in front, four behind, and an unspecified number on top; on busy days, presumably as many as could get on and keep on.

Wardell lived at Raindale Inn, about a quarter of a mile on the Levisham side of Raindale Mill, and here five horses were kept. A typical journey was somewhat as follows: the coach would leave Pickering with a driver and one horse, and the gradients being favourable, this sufficed to bring the coach to Raindale; here the horse was changed, and an additional one yoked tandem-wise with Wardell as postillion, who would go as far as Fen Bogs, practically the summit of the line. At this point the leading horse would be detached and go back to Raindale, the coach being taken on by the remaining horse to the incline top at Goathland. From the bottom of the incline the coach would run over the nearly level track for some distance by its own momentum, and if the wind were fair would get nearly to Grosmont, whence another horse took it on to Whitby.

On the return trip one horse would bring the coach to the foot of the incline at Beck Hole, and another from the bank top to Fen Bogs; thence it would run largely by itself to Raindale, where another horse would take it to Pickering.

If the weather was bad or wind contrary, the postillion and horse had to go and meet the coach, and help it over the awkward sections of the line. Postillions do not seem to have been employed for very long, the extra horse being attached as before, but driven from the coach.

Wardell afterwards became a plate-layer on the Y. & N.M.R. and the N.E.R., and now at the age of 78 still lives at Pickering in receipt of a pension from the N.E.R. after 55 years of work for the railway. I am pleased to be able to include a photogram of the old gentleman taken in June 1905, standing at the door of his abode, which adjoins the railway; so he is within sight and sound of the line to which he has devoted his life. (Fig. 14).

Two trains each way per day appear to have been the usual service provided. On the first train from Whitby, William Turnbull, of that town, officiated as guard to Pickering, and

Negative by] [*G. W. J. Potter.*
FIG. 14. W. WARDELL, A POSTILLION-RIDER.

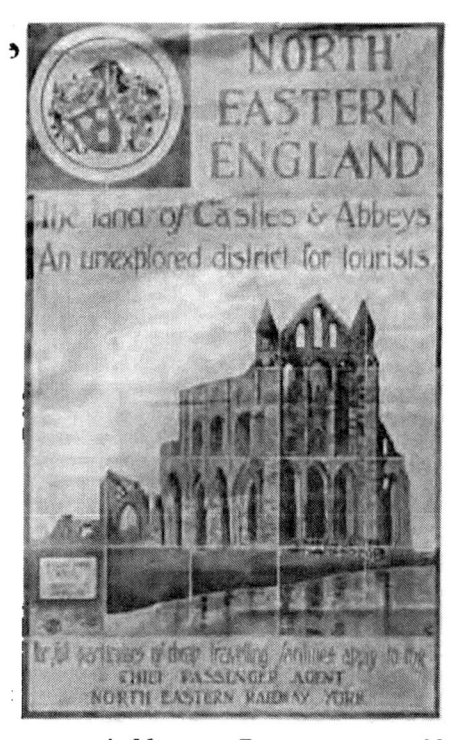

FIG. 15. A MODERN POSTER OF THE N.E.R.

proceeded thence to York in the same capacity on the stage coach; after a short interval he returned to Pickering, transferred himself to the railway, and reached Whitby again the same evening by the second train.

Communication between Scarborough and Whitby was obtained in a somewhat similar manner as witness the annexed notice :—

NEW COACH.

The Public are respectfully informed that the Queen a Four-Inside Coach, has commenced running from Scarborough to Pickering and Helmsley, Daily, (Sundays excepted.) The Queen leaves the George Inn, Scarboro', at Seven o'clock in the morning, reaching the Black Swan Inn, Pickering, at Half-past Nine o'clock, in time for the Railway Coach to Whitby; and, after the arrival of the Railway Coach from Whitby, it proceeds to the New Inn, Helmsley, arriving there at Twelve o'clock.

At Three o'clock in the afternoon, the same Coach leaves Helmsley for Pickering, at which place it arrives in time for the Railway Coach to Whitby, remaining at Pickering until the arrival of the Railway Coach from Whitby, and proceeds to Scarboro', arriving there at Ten o'clock.

N.B. Only two Coachmen and no guard.

Pickering, July 19, 1836.

Soon after the opening of the railway the company published a finely illustrated volume describing the scenery in the neighbourhood of the line. It has already been referred to in the Foreword, but it seems advisable to here give a somewhat fuller account of this interesting work.

The text was written by Mr. Henry Belcher, of the firm of Belcher & Walker, Solicitors, Whitby; and the illustrations were from drawings made by Mr. George Dodgson. A supplementary chapter describing the opening of the railway was written and contributed by Mr. Thomas Clark, the Treasurer.

March 1836, is given as the date of the introduction, and 30th May 1836, that of the account of the opening ceremonies, so presumably it was on sale about July of that year. There were six chapters, entitled: Whitby, Eskdale, Vale of Goathland, Newton Dale, Pickering, The Railway; and three appendices: the legendary account of the murder of a monk of Whitby; a list of the plants found in the district adjacent to the railway; an account of the opening.

Thirteen steel engravings on plate paper—and eight woodcuts in the text illustrated the volume, which appears to have been published in large and small paper editions at the respective prices of 15/- and 10/-.

The steel engravings are as follows:—

Whitby Abbey, North Aisle; Whitby from West Pier; Cliffs at Peak; Whitby Abbey from Churchyard; Sleights Bridge; Bridge in Eskdale, No. 5; Entrance to the Vale of Goathland; Thomason Foss; Entrance to Newton Dale; Newton Dale Scarrs; South Dale, Newton Dale; Raindale Mill; Pickering Castle.

All these views are on plate paper—thus differing from the woodcuts which are inserted in the text—but as the leaves are simply pasted in it is an easy matter to detach them; intending purchasers should therefore carefully examine the work to see that it is quite complete.

Although the volumes would probably be classed as royal and demy octavos, they are really quartos: the signatures being made up of four instead of eight leaves. The two sizes roughly speaking are $10\frac{1}{2}$ by $6\frac{1}{2}$ inches and 9 by $5\frac{1}{2}$ inches, outside measurement. The pagination is viii + 115, and date on title 1836. These notes should enable anyone who possesses the book to collate his copy, and see that it is complete. A few remaining copies, equal to new, were on sale in Whitby a few years ago, but none is now procurable, and in any case it is a scarce railway book, as are indeed most of the volumes on these early railways of about a similar date.

George Haydock Dodgson was born at Liverpool on 16th August 1811, and in due time was apprenticed to George Stephenson; he was thus brought into the Whitby district, and prepared the plans for this railway. Soon after 1836 he settled in London, where he was employed by several architects and by the proprietors of illustrated newspapers to make drawings for them. Ten views of the London & North Western Railway, published probably about 1845, appear to have been engraved by him after drawings by E. Radclyffe. Joining the New Society of Painters in Water Colours, he was elected an Associate exhibitor in 1842, but resigned in 1847 in order to join the older Society of Painters in Water Colours, and of which he became a full member in 1852. Whitby and Richmond (Yorks.) were favourite spots of his, and he paid many visits to each of these noted places of beauty. His death took place in London on 4th June 1880.

One of his paintings, The Lake Terrace, now hangs in the Leicester Museum.

Fig. 3 is a reproduction of the plate by Dodgson showing the entrance into Newton Dale; and lest it may be thought that the artist was gifted with a highly vivid imagination in depicting a rainbow in such a manner, a passage is quoted fron *The Evolution of an English Town*. This is a recent book giving an excellent account of the town of Pickering from the earliest times, and is written by Gordon Home, a well-known water-colour painter. He says

In a book published in 1836 . . . . a series of very delicate steel engravings of the wild scenery of Newton Dale were given. One of them shows the gorge under the deep gloom of a storm but relieved with the contrast of a rainbow springing from one side of the rocky walls. This effect may perhaps seem highly exaggerated, but on one occasion when I was exploring part of the Dale, between Levisham and Fen Bogs, I was astonished to see a brilliant rainbow backed by dense masses of indigo clouds and occupying precisely the position of the one shown in the old engraving. In such weather as this, when sudden rays of sunlight fall upon the steep slopes of bracken and heather and on the precipitous rocks above, the blazing colours seem almost unreal and the scenery suggests Scotland more than any other part of England.

An interesting account of the line is given in *A Handbook for Railway Travellers*, compiled by Edward Mogg, the third edition of which was published in 1846. After describing the course of the line from Bakehouse Lane, Pickering, the author remarks

The Whitby and Pickering Railway belongs not to the class that may be literally said to "annihilate both time and space," locomotive engines not being employed thereon, its inclination being unfavourable to the propelling power of that valuable machine, which, notwithstanding its astonishing capability, in cases of sudden elevation utterly fails; stationary engines are consequently made available in ascending the steeper acclivities, while upon the more gradual rise, the moderate descent and level portions of the line horses are employed; the visitors to the Whitby and Pickering Railway will nevertheless have no reason to regret the absence of a rapidity that will most assuredly detract from and very considerably diminish the interest of this delightful ride, the Railway passing as it does through a country unrivalled for the beauty and diversified nature of its scenery; upon this subject, however, the contracted space to which these remarks are necessarily confined, leave the Editor no room for enlargement, to those, therefore, who may feel inclined to doubt this assertion, he confidently refers for confirmation to a very beautiful work with plates, descriptive and illustrative of the very interesting country by which it is environed.

Not a bad length, Mr. Mogg, for one sentence.

In a foot-note it is stated that the railway is now wholly worked by locomotive power. As this event did not happen until 1847 it is probable that the date of the book should be somewhat later than 1846.

A table of distances is given by Mogg and is herewith transcribed :—

Pickering to	Miles.
The Newton Road	¾
Leavisham Brook	4¼
Newton and Leavisham Road	6
Raindale Mill	7
Saltersgate Brook	10
Fen Steps Summit	12¼
Goadland and Pickering Road	13¼
Goadland and Whitby Road	14½
Beck Hole	15½
Road from Growmond Bridge	17¼
Growmond Abbey	18
Esk Hall	21
Whitby and Pickering Road	21¼
Suspension Bridge	22½
Whitby	24

It will be observed that the old spelling of Leavisham, Goadland, and Growmond is adhered to, and it may be remarked that even at the present time when talking with natives of the district—more especially the old people—the two latter places are frequently given the pronunciation according with the above spelling.

On the map accompanying the book the route of the railway is drawn quite out of place between Whitby and Goathland.

CHAPTER III.

1836 TO 1853.

*Yorke, Yorke, for my monie,
Of all the Citties that ever I see,
For mery pastime and companie,
  Except the Cittie of London.*

W. Elderton, 1584.

LAST year (1905) *The Holiday Annual of the North Eastern Railway* was published at York on behalf of the company, with a view of attracting passengers to the various beautiful districts that are served by the railway. Among other interesting matter a map was given bearing the title 'THE FIRST RAILWAY MAP PUBLISHED. DATE 1836.' This proved to be a reproduction of a map that first appeared in the *Athenaeum*, (23rd Jan. 1836) and it is there stated to have been drawn specially for that journal by James Arrowsmith, a nephew of the elder Aaron Arrowsmith, the renowned cartographer.

Although it is not the first railway map that was published, it is probable that it was a very early, perhaps the earliest, map that gave a comprehensive view of the railway system. Such lines as were in operation about that time (1830-6) were shown on the large scale canal maps of both Walker and Bradshaw. Next to the stage-coaches of the road, the canal barges were the chief means of travel, and for the carriage of merchandize were actually more important; moreover the locomotive was a new-comer and hardly tested as yet, so it was not surprising that maps entirely devoted to the railways had not yet been published.

In the original map of 1836 the various railway lines are shown divided into three classes: those completed and in operation by a thick line; in progress of formation by a dotted line; and those projected by a thin hair-line. Unfortunately the foot-note to the map in the *Holiday Annual* transposes the two latter, and thus gives a totally wrong idea of the railway industry.

The little W. & P.R. is correctly indicated in the *Athenaeum* map as being in progress, and the following inaccurate, though amusing, description of the line appears in the text: 'The *Whitby and Pickering*, a coal railway of about 17 miles in extent, the cost of which may have been 120,000 *l*. It is a descent all the way from Pickering, and must be worked cheaply, as the waggons return empty from Whitby. A part of it has been recently finished.'

It is not possible now to give the history of the company as fully as could be wished, owing largely to the absence of any records; but several items of interest have been gathered together from various sources, and arranged in chronological order. By this means it is hoped that a fairly continuous account of the fortunes of the W. & P.R. may be obtained.

The Whitby Stone Company had been formed in 1834 by 24 Whitby gentlemen including Mr. Stephenson, and it was one of the first of the new enterprises brought into being by the opening of the railway. The quarries owned by the company were situated at Lease Rigg near Grosmont; the wharf and offices at Boghall; and a wharf, office, and agent were also provided at London. The first cargo of ironstone sent to the Birtley Iron Company, Middlesboro' was in 1836, and came from the Pecton seam at Grosmont.

In the first twelve months ending May 1836, upwards of 10,000 tons of stone were sent to Whitby for shipment to London.

The Grosmont Lime Company, with lime kilns near the Tunnel, was formed in 1836; the limestone being brought from Pickering. Two companies for supplying the latter town with sea-borne coal imported at Whitby were likewise in operation about this time. Two years later a Brick and Tile Works was started near Ruswarp, and other industries were soon in operation. In 1839 the Wylam Iron Company commenced mining operations at Grosmont. A period of depression in trade followed, a revival commencing in 1845, and in the next year the world-famed firm of Bolckow, Vaughan, & Co., of Middlesboro', became purchasers of the Grosmont ore. For a long time nearly all the ironstone that was mined in Cleveland came from this place; and was conveyed by rail to Whitby, thence being shipped to the ironworks. By 1850 the richer beds of iron ore in North Cleveland had been discovered, and Grosmont's day of prosperity as a mining centre was soon after at an end.

At the close of 1836 it was stated that the traffic upon the railway generally had exceeded the calculations, and more than realised the hopes, of the projectors. The exact number of passengers conveyed along the line in the July of that year was 3,903, and in August about 4,200. The gross receipts for the four months ending in October were equal to 9% per annum on the paid-up capital. It was pointed out that the number of

Negative by]   *[G. W. J. Potter.*

FIG. 16. No. 557 APPROACHING KIRBY.

Negative by]   *[G. W. J. Potter.*

FIG. 17. KIRBY, OR BLACK BULL: A DISUSED STATION.

passengers taken had been greater in proportion to the previous communication between the two termini than upon any other line of railway. Perhaps this was hardly a fair comparison, as travelling over these Yorkshire moors is none too pleasant other than in the summer months, and doubtless people who were obliged to journey between Whitby and Pickering hailed with delight the facilities provided for them.

Even those who had their own carriages appear to have sometimes preferred the charming ride through the valley of the Esk and Newton Dale to the laborious climb and somewhat rough travelling over the moors, as witness the following account of Mr. Chapman's return from Whitby on his way home to Woodford.

'On Thursday, 29 September 1836, the first gentleman's carriage was sent up the line on a truck, with its owner and his two daughters in it. It was the travelling carriage of Abel Chapman, Esq., of Woodford, in Essex. Mr. Chapman is uncle to Aaron Chapman, Esq., M.P., and one of the oldest natives of Whitby, being in the 86th year of his age. He appeared to be in excellent health and spirits, and was exceedingly delighted with so novel a mode of travelling, as well as with the beautiful scenery through which he was conveyed; contrasting no doubt with what he would recollect of the mountainous ascents, rugged roads and dreary wastes which he had to pass in making the same journey at former periods. Any man of his years, who could bear the fatigue, and who recollected things as they were in his youth, could not but be well repaid for the trouble and expense of a journey from the south, by witnessing changes so great—improvements so extraordinary—even supposing he had had no other object in view in visiting his native town.'

An accident—fortunately unattended with loss of life—occurred on 3rd December at the Goathland incline. The coach from Pickering was being lowered down the bank when the rope broke: fortunately the man who had charge of the wagons ascending, which were attached to the other end of the rope, was able to lock the wheels and so prevent their running down the hill. The driver and guard of the passenger coach retained their presence of mind and were able to check the speed of the runaway; they did not alarm the passengers, and few were aware that they had been in considerable danger.

Heavy falls of snow during the last weeks of 1836 rendered the roads in the neighbourhood impassable for the coaches running to Guisboro and Scarborough, considerably delayed the Pickering mail coach, and stopped all communication to and from Whitby and the surrounding districts. The railway coaches, however, continued to run at the stated times, and do not appear to have been delayed more than an hour in performing the entire journey.

This was a great surprise to the public, who had thought that snow would prove fatal to the running of the coaches, and naturally the spirits of the proprietors were greatly elated by the success of their venture.

It will not occasion surprise to learn that the construction of the railway was made a political object, and that it gave an opportunity for the two sides to fiercely denounce each other. A profusion of letters, not always in the best of taste, appeared in the local papers. It would be useless to reproduce even a tithe of them, so an editorial from the Liberal point of view—far more temperate than usual—and a letter from a Conservative writer should suffice to show the state of affairs.

We believe it is generally allowed that the undertaking of the W. & P.R. sprang out of the contested election that occurred on the enfranchisement of Whitby; and but for that circumstance no such Railway would now have been in existence. The Liberal party never advocated the formation of the line as a final measure. The getting a level road into the interior of the country, (the chief difficulty once surmounted) its ultimately answering a good purpose, by a further extension, they did not doubt; but during the depression that marked the period of the first election for the Borough, the bulk of the community cared and knew little further than that Railroads had benefitted other places; and, therefore, threw up their hats, and exclaimed, "A Whitby and Pickering Railroad for ever!" The principal shareholders are mostly Conservatives, and formerly scouted the idea of such an undertaking; and more recently, some of them have expressed their conviction of the superior utility of a number of Joint Stock Whale Fishing ships, belonging to the port; probably the latter might have afforded a more permanent source of influence in the support of Toryism in the Borough. The W. & P.R. is eminently a Tory speculation, and is at present very generally viewed as an engine to support Conservative principles.

An extract from the letter alluded to now follows :—

The W. & P.R., which has benefitted both places, though perhaps not to the full extent its projectors wished, owes its exertions to Robert Campion, whose munificent sum of £5,000, at the head of the list of shareholders, baffled the subterfuge of sham supporters of the measure, and compelled them to act up to their professions, and when a body of men offer their purses in aid of any public undertaking, likely to renovate the falling fortunes of Whitby, in barter for the political support of the electors, I feel no scruples in insisting upon the fulfilment of their part of the contract.

Although the railway was completed, and was so far successful, the financial portion of the scheme was in anything but a satisfactory condition. As we have seen, £80,000 was the most that could be raised in the neighbourhood, and it was hoped by exercising rigid economy in the construction to complete the work for that amount; this however was not found possible, owing to various causes largely beyond the control of the company. Mr. Belcher's account of the situation is terse and to the point, and is as follows:—

> This sum [£80,000] included land for only a single line of railway, and contained no allowance for land and buildings at the termini, or the means of conveying goods and passengers. Iron too, at the time this estimate was made, was but one half the price it has since attained.
>
> The Directors, having every reason to anticipate the necessity of a double line ere many years shall have elapsed, secured the requisite land for the purpose in the first instance, and have also expended several thousand pounds in the purchase of land and buildings at each of the termini, and in providing coaches, waggons, horses, and other conveniences for working the line. Abstracting, therefore, as may very fairly be done, the cost of these several items from the total expenditure, it will be found that the actual cost of the railway, notwithstanding the continued advance in the price of iron, has not much exceeded the original estimate.

The expense of making the line worked out at about £4,400 per mile, or a total of £105,600 for the 24 miles; this being slightly over double the estimate of Stephenson.

At a meeting held towards the close of 1836, it was stated that the company were in debt to the extent of £13,000; and three proposals were brought forward for consideration.

1. To advance £20 per share.
2. To apply to Parliament to borrow more money.
3. To let the working of the line.

However no definite conclusion was then arrived at.

As the shares of the company were at 50% discount, and two gentlemen who had been directors had recently parted with their holdings of £500 and £600 on these terms, it was felt that the choice lay between the second and third schemes. Many were in favour of letting the working of the line, but at a subsequent meeting in January 1837, it was decided to obtain powers from Parliament to raise an additional capital of £30,000.

Accordingly this was done, and the bill received the Royal Assent on the 5th May 1837. It was a fairly short Act (28 sections), and beyond the financial authorisation and revision of rates, there was little of importance in it.

Another favourable report was presented by the directors towards the close of 1837, after an experience of nearly a year and a half in working the line. Therein we read that a great increase had taken place in the tonnage, amount of traffic, and number of passengers conveyed on the line during the last half-year—the increase of the latter being 8,000 and the former 6,000 tons over the previous six months; and that had there been a greater number of wagons available for the conveyance of goods, this augmentation to the business of the company would have been still greater.

As the foundation stone of St. Matthew's Church, Grosmont, was to be laid on the 16th September, 1840, the railway authorities issued a notification to the effect that carriages would be ready at the Whitby Station from 10.0 a.m. to 12.0 noon or a quarter after, to convey passengers at the usual fares to the Tunnel Inn; where, between the hours of 12 and 1, the company had been requested to assemble, the ceremony beginning at the latter hour. Mr. Henry Belcher had taken the lead in the scheme for the erection of a church, aiding the work in many ways, and had the gratification of seeing the completion and opening of the building in 1842. Upon his death in 1854 a five lancet window of stained glass was inserted in the church as a memorial to him. A fellow townsman says 'His benevolence and urbanity, with a refined taste and intelligence, gained him the general esteem.'

A second edition of Dr. George Young's *Picture of Whitby* was published in 1840, and in its pages the author mentions that since the opening of the railway, there has been a daily coach to York, a coach twice a day to Pickering, and a coach daily to the Tunnel; also that a wagon with goods for Pickering and York runs daily by the railway.

This is not a particularly lucid statement: as firstly, there was then no communication with York by rail, the line terminating at Pickering; and secondly, it is stated that there are two coaches to Pickering and yet only one to the Tunnel—but the Tunnel having to be passed by all coaches going to Pickering, the easiest and most probable solution appears to be that there were three coaches in the day to the Tunnel, and that two only went all the way to Pickering.

The account given in the book is mixed up with the coaches running along the turnpike roads, and as the same word 'coach' is employed in each case, it makes it somewhat difficult to discover the true state of things from the learned Doctor's account.

Although the course of the W. & P.R. had been shown on the earliest of Bradshaw's railway maps (1839), and in the maps of his celebrated guide, it was not until May 1843, that any reference to the railway was made in its pages. In that issue however it is stated that the line is worked by horse-power, and the following details are given: 'From York to Pickering a coach daily, (Sundays excepted), and from Pickering by railway to Whitby, leaving York at 12, on the arrival of the trains from the South, East, and West, and arriving at Whitby at 6 p.m. From Whitby to Pickering by railway, and thence to York by coach daily, (Sundays excepted), leaving Whitby at 8½ a.m., and reaching York at 2½ p.m., in time for the trains going South, East, and West to London, Derby, Hull, Leeds, Liverpool, &c.

'There is a luggage train daily between Whitby and Pickering, by which passengers may be conveyed at a lower rate of fares, this train leaves Whitby at 2 p.m., and arrives at Pickering at 6 p.m., and the one from Pickering leaves at 12 noon.'

The ordinary fares from Whitby to Pickering were 4/- inside and 3/- outside, and from Whitby to York 13/- and 8/- respectively.

Notwithstanding the creditable amount of traffic carried since the opening of the railway, and the encouraging reports that had been issued, it was patent to all that an isolated line like the W. & P.R. could not be a financial success until it was joined to a larger line, and thus enabled to become a portion of a through route. The question was therefore: with which company should it amalgamate—the Stockton & Darlington, or the York & North Midland? Neither was yet within some miles, but the S. & D. were extending their line from Middlesborough to Redcar, while the Y. & N.M. obtained an Act in 1844 for the construction of a railway between York and Scarborough with a branch to Pickering. After careful consideration it was decided that the interests of the proprietors would be best served by the sale of the undertaking to the Y. & N.M. company.

The celebrated George Hudson was then Chairman of the latter line; he had paid a visit to Whitby in 1835 when the railway was being made, and had obtained an introduction to George Stephenson. Doubtless he would clearly remember the quaint little horse line when conducting negotiations with its directors. Subject to the consent of Parliament the sale was agreed to, the purchase money being fixed at £80,000, considerably less than it had cost the shareholders to build the railway.

In July 1844 the first coach was altered to leave Whitby at 7 a.m., and passengers were due to arrive at York at 12.30 p.m.

During the three summer months (July, August, September) a first class coach left Pickering at 11 a.m., was due to arrive at Whitby at 1.30 p.m., and returned thence at 4 p.m.

At the half-yearly meeting held at Whitby in October, 1844, Thomas Fishburn, who was in the chair, said 'the returns for the six months ending 9th October, had most materially increased upon the returns for the corresponding period ending in October 1843. Further, from the improvement that is arising in trade and shipping generally, and from the great desire evinced by strangers to visit the beautiful and romantic neighbourhood of Whitby, there is every reason to suppose that the Whitby & Pickering Railway, when conjoined with the York and Scarborough line, will become a prosperous undertaking.'

Application was made in due course for the necessary powers, the bill being read for the first time on 7th February, and receiving the Royal Assent on 30th June 1845. It authorised the sale of the Whitby & Pickering Railway to the York & North Midland Company, likewise the raising of £135,400 with borrowing powers to the extent of £45,000. Leave was given for the employment of locomotive engines, and the route was to be deviated and altered with a view to its improvement and suitability for steam traction; the work to be completed within five years. Some of the rates were revised, and while section 33 allows a 5 mile minimum, section 35 fixes the fares for passengers at 3d., 2d., and 1½d. per mile for the three classes with an optional 6 mile minimum. First class passengers were allowed 150 lbs., second and third class 100 lbs., of personal luggage free of charge.

Contracts for the alteration of the line were soon published, and in a short time men were at work on the line.

The railway from York to Scarborough was opened on 7th July 1845. The August service between the two places consisted of four trains in each direction on week days and one on Sundays. By October the passenger service between Rillington and Pickering was also in active operation.

Some interesting particulars can be gleaned from a return that was presented to the House of Commons in August 1846, showing the amount of passenger duty that had been paid to the Government by the various railway companies of England and Wales during the period extending from the 1st September 1845 to 5th July 1846. The highest amount was that of the London & Birmingham, £25,317/2/2; this being followed by the Great Western with £24,749/17/6; after a big drop the Grand Junction with £12,911/1/8; then other companies—49 in all—with smaller amounts. At the bottom of the list come four isolated little lines, and the pride of place—unfortunately at the wrong end, however—belongs, unwillingly enough we may be sure, to the W. & P.R.

The companies are

Bodmin & Wadebridge	4 15	0
Stratford & Moreton	3 16	1½
Hereford & Monmouth Gap ...	2 0	0
Whitby & Pickering	1 19	6¾

As the passenger duty was at the rate of 5% it follows that the total sum received by the W. & P.R. from their passengers during the period (44 weeks) was only £39/11/3, or less than a pound per week. Even allowing for the inclusion of the two summer months, July and August, it is doubtful whether the total year's receipts would exceed £60, a very meagre amount for passenger traffic. If the number of passengers carried during the year ending June 1842, namely 13,441, be taken and each fare reckoned at a penny only, this will amount to not less than £56; and will thus give some idea of the drop that had been experienced. The contributing cause was probably the disorganisation and perhaps complete stoppage of the service, consequent upon the alteration of the line that was then taking place, with a view of preparing it for the forth-coming steam-drawn trains.

June 1847 witnessed the opening of the Whitby & Pickering under its new conditions of a double line of railway worked by locomotives; not now as an independent concern, but as a branch of that growing company, the York & North Midland Railway. The first locomotive entered the town on the afternoon of Friday, the 4th of June. The first station at Whitby—such as it was—had been erected on the site of a ship-building yard belonging to Messrs. Fishburn and Broderick, and was located near the present engine house. The new one occupied the space formerly utilised by Messrs. Barry and Barrick for two other ship-yards, conclusively proving the important part that was played by Whitby in the building of wooden ships in the olden days. Other stations were erected along the line, most of them remaining to the present day, and in many cases the buildings are but little altered.

Upon the linking-up of the railways between Pickering, Rillington, and York, and consequent through communication by steam, the necessity for the stage-coaches disappeared, and it was not long before they were taken off the road altogether. Many of the guards and drivers obtained employment in various capacities on the railway. One named Sedman, who was originally a guard on the coach to York, became a passenger guard on the North Eastern, a post which he retained for several years; and in the performance of his duties was destined to take a leading part in the unfortunate accident at the Goathland incline in 1864. Upon his retirement from active service he took up his abode in the pleasant old town of Pickering, residing there till his death.

Originally there were three stations between Rillington and Pickering: Low Marishes, High Marishes, and Black Bull; the latter being sometimes known as Kirby or Kirby Misperton from the village of that name distant about three miles. Soon afterwards two of these three stations, Low Marishes and Black

Bull, were closed; the probable cause being that there was not sufficient traffic to warrant their retention. The remaining one appears in maps of about that date as High Marishes, Marishes, and Marishes Road; the latter being the official name, and it occurs as such in a Y. & N.M.R. Rule Book for 1852.

The station buildings of Black Bull or Kirby still remain, and their present-day aspect is shown in the photogram taken in July 1905, and reproduced in Figs. 16 & 17. The name of the station was derived from the sign of a public-house which stands on the high road opposite the end of the station approach. In the distance may be seen a signal-cabin, this is situated at the intersection of the high road and the railroad, and is known as Black Bull Crossing. The curious looking signal by the station buildings, though not employed for ordinary working, is occasionally brought into use for an especial purpose. Thus should it be desired for a farm-waggon, traction engine, or similar heavy vehicle to cross the line, it is the duty of the person in charge of the vehicle to turn the signal so as to show the face of the board to all approaching trains; when the crossing is clear the pole is moved round and the narrow edge of the board is once more presented to passing trains. Several of these signals are still in position on this section of the N.E.R.

In 1847, Mr. Aaron Chapman, who had represented the Borough of Whitby since its creation in 1832, retired from public life, and the electors invited Robert Stephenson to champion their interests in Parliament: to this proposal he consented, and was unanimously chosen on 30th July, retaining the seat until his death in 1859.

Now that Whitby possessed through railway communication with York, and thence to other parts of England, Hudson next conceived the idea of turning the erstwhile shipbuilding town into a fashionable watering-place, and to this end purchased in 1848 the West Cliff fields. The Royal Hotel and several terraces of lodging-houses were then built, streets planned, and the road called the Khyber Pass constructed to afford an easy access to the riverside, harbour, and shore. Upon his downfall soon after, the estate passed into the hands of the railway authorities, afterwards being acquired by Sir George Elliot, whose son, Sir Charles, is now the owner. George Street and Hudson Street still remain on the West Cliff as memories of the 'Railway King.'

The first detailed time-table of the services between York, Scarborough, and Whitby giving all the stations and showing the departure and arrival times appears in *Bradshaw* for July 1848; the previous issues having only shown the times at the terminal points.

Negative by] [*G. W. J. Potter.*
FIG. 18. THE NEW TUNNEL, GROSMONT.

Negative by] [*G. W. J. Potter.*
FIG. 19. GROSMONT STATION.

PICKERING RAILWAY.

Appended are the revised times for August 1848 as far as they can be deciphered, for truth to tell the times given in the usually immaculate *Bradshaw* are somewhat contradictory, and not always capable of satisfactory adjustment.

	1.2.3.	1.2.Mail.	1.2.3.	1.2.Gov.	1.2.3.	1.2.Ex.	1.2.3.
York		7.0		9.15	12.0	4.0	5.30
Malton		8.0		10.15	1.0	4.45	6.30
Rillington Junc.	8.0	—	10.3	—	1.20	5.10	6.55
Marishes Road	8.10	—	10.13	—	1.30	5.15	7.5
Pickering ...	8.20	8.30	10.23	10.50	1.40	5.30	7.10
Levisham ...		8.45			2.0		7.25
Goathland ...		9.15			2.25		7.55
Grosmont ...		9.40			2.50		8.15
Sleights ...		9.50			2.55		8.25
Ruswarp ...		9.55			3.0		8.30
Whitby ...		10.0			3.5		8.35

On Sundays the 7.0 a.m. Mail from York was the only train.

The single fares from York were as follows:—

Miles.		1st.	2nd.	3rd.
21¼	Malton ...	5/0	3/6	2/6
25¾	Rillington ...	6/0	4/0	3/0
32¼	Pickering ...	8/0	5/6	4/0
56¼	Whitby ...	12/0	9/6	7/0

Return Fares are not shown, but it is probable that return tickets at a slight reduction were issued for first and second class passengers only; no such facilities being available for either the third or government class traveller.

Trains from Whitby were run according to the annexed table.

	1.2.Gov.	1.2.3.	1.2.3.	1.2.Mail.	1.2.3.
Whitby ...		7.45	11.15	3.15	
Ruswarp ...		7.50	11.20	3.20	
Sleights ...		7.55	11.30	3.30	
Grosmont ...		8.5	11.40	3.40	
Goathland ...		8.20	12.0	4.0	
Levisham ...		8.55	12.30	4.30	
Pickering ...	7.20	9.15	12.45	4.45	4.55
Marishes Road	7.30	9.25	1.0	—	5.5
Rillington Junc.	7.48	9.48	1.18	5.0	5.15
Malton ...	8.0	10.0	1.30	5.10	
York ...	9.5	11.0	2.30	6.10	

The Sunday service was provided by the running of the 3.15 p.m. from Whitby, reaching York a few minutes later than on week-days.

During the winter months the week-day trains were reduced to two each way between Whitby and Pickering.

Kirby first appears as a station in the issue of *Bradshaw* for November 1853.

About the year 1853 the three principal railway companies possessing territory in the North and East of Yorkshire—the York, Newcastle, & Berwick, the York & North Midland, and the Leeds Northern—being heartily tired of the ruinous competition with each other in which they had been indulging, decided that their better plan was to work harmoniously together, and to this end drew up a scheme of amalgamation. A bill for this purpose was presented to Parliament by the Y.N. & B., as being the largest of the three companies, and it received the Royal Assent on 31st July 1854.

The title of the new undertaking was henceforth the North Eastern Railway.

Sixty-eight Acts of Parliament were recited in the Amalgamation Act. The total mileage of the combined companies, namely 725½ miles, was greater than that then possessed by any other company; and the capital of the new corporation was about 23 millions sterling.

Many lines have been absorbed since then, and the mileage of the N.E.R. at the close of 1905 is stated to be 1695 miles; and the total distance run over by their trains throughout that year totalled 26,429,547 miles. The capital had grown to £76,986,571; the receipts for that year were £9,407,930; and the expenditure £5,940,990.

2000 engines; 4461 coaching vehicles, and 99,845 goods vehicles comprised the rolling stock; and for a graphical view of the growth of each individual unit, the reader is referred to Fig. 41.

CHAPTER IV.

1854 to 1905.

Behold! I come with lightning speed
   Along my shining track of steel,
And underneath my thundering tread
   The old earth seems to rack and reel.
O'er hill and dale, through fertile vale,
   I sweep along and never tire,
With limbs that never felt a pulse,
   And breath of living flame and fire.

The country village and the town
   By me are linked; are joined together;
And natives of the dingy streets
   May rove by me amongst the heather.
Great cities that are parted wide
   By mountains, valleys, plains, and streams,
By me are to each other joined,
   With all their commerce, wealth, and schemes.

W. Hampson.

IT may be remembered that one William Thompson published a pamphlet in 1833, advocating a railway from Whitby to Pickering; when the line was completed he was appointed station-master at the former place. In July 1854—having then left the service—he issued another work entitled *Remarks in favour of the North Yorkshire and Cleveland Railway*. The royal assent for this company's bill had been given on the 9th of July; and Thompson goes on to say that having had 20 years' experience in railway matters, he believes that the projected line from Grosmont to Picton on the Leeds Northern—formerly Leeds & Thirsk—will pay a good interest and benefit Whitby. Having been connected with the management of the W. & P. for nearly 10 years he attributes the loss sustained by that company to the employment of horse-power. To take lots of 120 tons of ironstone from Grosmont to Whitby in the old days required 20 horses under the charge of 10 men; the journey both ways occupied 4 hours; and the cost was 1/6 per wagon holding 4 tons, or a total of £2/5/-

'Now, the York & North Midland make no charge for haulage, and the ordinary dues are rather less than when horses were employed; but even if the company should add the cost of haulage, the total rate would not exceed 9/-, thus leaving a balance in favour of steam of £1/16/0 out of every £2/5/0; furthermore, the double journey would be completed in one hour instead of four hours.

'As the Scarboro and York railway was not then made there was no through communication, and such traffic had to be transferred to coach.' He states that 'the Directors, after allowing for current expenses, paid £2,600 to bond-holders, £1,800 of which was received from mineral and other traffic between Grosmont and Whitby.' However, he is of opinion that the company would have done better if they had made a line to Danby instead of Pickering, so naturally he welcomes the newcomer which proposes to serve that district.

The *Whitby Gazette* made its first appearance on the 6th of July, 1854, and was primarily, not much more than a list of the visitors then in the town. Thirteen numbers only were published that year, and the same quantity in the following year; in each case during the season, July to September. Afterwards it developed into the orthodox newspaper, and as such has continued uninterruptedly and successfully to the present day, being now carried on by the sons of the original founder. From its columns items of interest relating to the railway have been extracted, and these form the basis of much of the matter in the next few pages; indeed in many cases this is the only source of information for such local news.

In the first issue the complete service for July 1854 is shown, this being as follows:—

Miles.		1, 2, Gov. a.m.	1, 2 p.m.	Mail. 1, 2, 3 p.m.	Sunday. 1, 2 Gov. p.m.
—	Whitby ....dep.	8 0	12 45	4 0	4 0
1½	Ruswarp .... ,,	8 5	12 50	4 5	4 5
3	Sleights .... ,,	8 10	12 55	4 10	4 10
6¼	Grosmont .... ,,	8 20	1 5	4 20	4 20
9¼	Goathland .... ,,	8 40	1 25	4 40	4 40
18	Levisham............... ,,	9 5	1 50	5 5	5 5
24	Pickering .... ,,	9 20	2 5	5 20	5 20
—	Kirby .... ,,	9 25	2 10	5 25	5 25
27½	Marishes Road .... ,,	9 30	2 15	5 30	5 30
30½	Rillington Junction ......arr.	9 40	2 25	5 40	5 40
47	Scarboro............... ,,	11 40	4 25	6 30	—
56¾	York............... ,,	11 0	3 45	7 0	7 0

Negative by] [*G. H. J. Potter.*

FIG. 20. GOATHLAND STATION.

Negative by] [*G. W. J. Potter.*

FIG. 21. SLEIGHTS STATION.

Miles.			Mail. 1, 2, Gov. a.m.	1, 2 a.m.	1, 2, 3 p.m.	Sunday. 1, 2, Gov. a.m.
—	York	...dep.	6 0	9 40	4 30	6 0
—	Scarboro	,,	—	10 20	5 5	—
26¼	Rillington Junction	,,	7 18	10 55	5 50	7 18
29¼	Marishes Road	,,	7 25	11 0	5 57	7 25
—	Kirby	,,	7 30	11 5	6 2	7 30
32¾	Pickering	,,	7 35	11 15	6 10	7 35
38¾	Levisham	,,	7 50	11 30	6 25	7 50
47½	Goathland	,,	8 20	11 57	6 51	8 20
50¼	Grosmont	,,	8 40	12 12	7 15	8 40
53¾	Sleights	,,	8 50	12 20	7 25	8 50
55¼	Ruswarp	.,	8 55	12 25	7 30	8 55
56¾	Whitby	arr.	9 0	12 30	7 35	9 0

The connecting times are also shewn to and from Hull, Leeds, and Normanton.

In the issue for 3rd August the first train leaves Whitby at 7.45 a.m.; and in that for the 31st August, four trains arrive at Whitby instead of the three that ran in July. Thus the 5.50 p.m. from Rillington Junction is cancelled, another (1, 2) leaves there at 4 p.m., calling at all places except Kirby and reaching Whitby at 5.40 p.m.; and the last (1, 2, 3) leaves Rillington at 7.12 p.m. and is due at Whitby at 9 p.m.

In 1855 Day Pleasure Trips were run by ordinary trains on Mondays, Wednesdays, and Fridays from Whitby to Scarboro and *vice versa*. During this and the following year the train service consisted of four trains in and the same number out of Whitby on week-days, and one each way on Sundays.

The following advertisement appeared in the issue of 8th August, 1857:—

> N.E.R. NOTICE.—The public are respectfully informed, that in consequence of an Accident to a Bridge, each of the Passenger Trains will leave Whitby half-an-hour earlier than at present advertised. This arrangement will commence to-morrow, August 8th, and will be continued until further notice.
>
> A. CHRISTISON,
> *General Passenger Superintendent.*

During the summer of 1857 the service of trains was improved, five being run from Rillington to Whitby, three of which did not call at Marishes Road, Kirby, or Levisham, but of course these were first and second only and thus did not benefit the third class passenger. The first train each way was first, second, and government, and one of the afternoon trains in each direction also took third class passengers. It may be as well to here point out that the distinction between the third and government classes was not always purely nominal, as in many cases in various parts of England the third class fare was higher than that allowed to be charged by the Government regulations, namely, one penny per mile. However this distinction gradually disappeared, as did the express fares which were once fairly general, and thus in place of the seven single fares (1, 2, 3, Gov., and Exp. 1, 2, 3) in use, there are now two, first and third, the second class being still retained on a few lines. Reverting to the train service of 1857 we find that there were five trains from Whitby, but the last leaving at 6.30 p.m. only went as far as Levisham. For the convenience of those attending Whitby market a train left at 2.55 p.m. on Saturdays only for all stations to Goathland. On Sundays the mail came in at 9 a.m. as on week-days and went out at 5 p.m. A train also left Whitby at 7.30 a.m. for Grosmont, returning from that place at 5.55 p.m. and reaching Whitby at 6.15 p.m., thus enabling intending passengers to leave Whitby and return thereto by train, a thing impossible with the present Sunday timing as both of the trains entering the town arrive in the early morning.

The bridge at Grosmont, originally built for carrying the horse railway over the Murk Esk was taken down at the end of October, 1858. A new one with a span of 60 feet and intended for the use of foot-passengers only was erected in its place, and opened on the 6th of November; the change being accomplished in a week.

On the first day of January, 1859, the undertaking of the North Yorkshire & Cleveland Railway Company passed into the hands of the North Eastern, and became a portion of their rapidly increasing system.

'On Saturday, 6th August, 1859 as the mid-day train was passing over Fen Bogs, the engine got off the line. The brakes were promptly applied, and although the engine went into the bog, and dragged two of the carriages after it, the train was brought to a stand with scarcely any inconvenience to the passengers. The stoker was partly covered with coke, but as soon as extricated he ran back to the top of the incline to get assistance, and after some little delay the passengers were forwarded to York by another engine, (the lady passenger occupying the interval by taking sketches), none of the carriages being much damaged. The engine was dug out and replaced on the line on Tuesday. It is cause for gratitude that no serious accident has occurred to any passengers on the Whitby and Pickering line since it was opened in May, 1836.'

At the half-yearly meeting of the North-Eastern Railway held on 10th August, 1860, the chairman, Mr. H. S. Thompson alluded to the importance of fully opening out the watering place of Whitby, saying they had done all that could be done for Scarboro, but little or nothing for Whitby, which he had no doubt might be made to yield an equally profitable return, for it evidently possessed the same natural advantages. At present, there was a serious obstacle to the traffic upon the Whitby and Pickering line, owing to the steep incline at Goathland. No person has ever been injured at that incline, but there was a fear of danger felt by the public. The incline was a great hindrance and inconvenience to the traffic, and it was deemed advisable to apply a remedy for the existing state of things.

'An estimate had been formed of the expense that would be incurred by making a deviation in the line to avoid the incline, and the sum named was £50,000. The extra expense at present incurred at the incline in wages, in locomotive powers, and other matters would be avoided, and the interest of the £50,000 would be fully saved. By avoiding the incline the company would be enabled to have excursion trains on the line, which they were not able to do under existing circumstances. He was of opinion that the work ought to be carried out as recommended by the directors, in connection with the completion of the remaining portion of the line from Castleton to Grosmont.

'The advantage derived by developing the traffic on the Scarboro Railway had been so great, that he thought it would be desirable to make an endeavour to bring out the Whitby traffic, which could not be effected without the incline were done away with.'

These suggestions were evidently adopted by the shareholders, as on 17th November, 1860 the Directors gave notice to apply next session for powers to complete the North Yorkshire & Cleveland line from the present terminus near Castleton to Grosmont; and to do away with the incline and fixed engine, by making a deviation in the Whitby & Pickering Railway, commencing about half-a-mile on the Goathland side of the tunnel and diverging to the left of the present line for about 4½ miles, going round the hill and joining the line again near Fen Bogs. Also for the power to purchase the parcels of ground occupied as a timber yard and pond by Mr. Edward Corner, and that portion of the Boghall Quay situate between the ford and Messrs. Turnbull and Sons' dock.

The death of Robert Stephenson on 12th October, 1859, left Whitby without a Parliamentary representative, and three candidates aspired for this honour. George Hudson was one, but he retired before the election, leaving T. Chapman, a descendant of Whitby's original member, to represent the Conservatives; and H. S. Thompson, the chairman of the N.E.R., as the Liberal candidate. The latter was successful, and was the first Liberal that had been returned for the borough.

Castleton station on the N.Y. & C. line was opened on the 1st April, 1860.

In June, 1861, we read that 'the N.E.R. have taken a liberal step in the right direction by this month granting two trains, the first and last in and out of Whitby, on week-days, at government fares.'

The Royal Assent was given to the Castleton & Grosmont extension and Whitby & Pickering deviation bill on 11th July, 1861. Three months later (12th October) between 5 and 6 p.m. a mineral train of four stone wagons was being drawn up the incline, and was nearly at the top, when the rope broke. The brakesman screwed down the brake, jumped out, and attempted to sprag the wheels but failed, so the trucks raced down the bank and ran into a goods train which had been shunted to allow the mail to pass. Fortunately nobody was hurt or killed. A week after a memorial was presented to the directors of the N.E.R., praying them to press on the works of the deviation, and thus avoid the possibility of an accident occurring at the incline to a passenger train.

By March 1862 the engineers had completed the survey of the line between Castleton and Grosmont, and were then engaged on the deviation, and in June 1862 the following advertisement appeared in the *Whitby Gazette*.

> The Directors are prepared to receive Tenders for constructing a Deviation line of Railway at Goathland on the Whitby and Pickering Branch, about 4½ miles long, commencing a little to the N.E. of the 50th mile post and terminating about the 45¾ mile post from York.
>
> J. CLEGHORN, SEC.

During the summer of 1862 five passenger trains each way ran between Rillington and Whitby, and about this time all these trains were extended to Malton, passengers being required to change there instead of at Rillington as formerly.

In October it is stated that the contractor (Mr. Nelson) is entering with spirit upon the railway extension, and that a commencement has been made with the deviation upon which are some very heavy works.

A survey was made during 1863 for a Coast line to connect the towns of Whitby and Scarboro, but many years were to elapse ere this became an accomplished fact.

The first serious accident to be recorded in connection with the line took place on the evening of 10th February, 1864, at the Goathland incline: two persons being killed and thirteen more or less injured thereby. The train to which the mishap occurred was the last from Malton and was due to leave there at 7.55 p.m., the real time of departure on this occasion being 8.1 p.m. Mr. W. Pickering was driver and Mr. J. Sedman guard, and the train duly arrived at the incline top. Here the usual practice was to detach the engine, run it round to the rear of the train, and then gently push the carriages—in one or more lots according to the number of them—over the brow of the incline on to the incline brake-van, to which was attached the rope from the engine-house. The train and the van having been coupled together, the rope was then paid out slowly and the train descended the bank, a check being kept on the speed by the incline guard who rode in the incline brake-van.

On this occasion the rope snapped, and all the weight of the train was thus only held in check by the brake of the incline van; the speed increased rapidly, and the rails being covered with ice and snow the brake failed to check the onward course of the train. Nearing the bottom the van left the rails, and the carriages following, all were overturned. The two victims, who were riding in the first-class carriage, were commercial travellers returning after their day's work to Whitby.

The coroner's jury brought in the following verdict:—

That the deceased John Mickle and William Torry accidentally came by their deaths whilst travelling on the Whitby branch of the North Eastern Railway, between Malton and Whitby, on the night of Wednesday, the 10th instant, by the breaking of the rope attached to the incline brake-van on the Goathland incline, and that in the opinion of the jury the rope was so much worn as to be unfit for the duty in which it was employed, and they cannot but express their surprise and regret that there appears to have been no systematic or efficient examination of the said rope by the superior officers of the company.

Of course there was an inquiry held by the Board of Trade who appointed Captain Tyler to conduct it. It was found that the rope—which was made of wire having six strands, each with a small hemp core—had been in use for 27 months and 2 days. It was 4½ inches in circumference; 1580 yards long; and weighed 112 cwt. 2 qrs., or 16 lbs. per fathom. The usual custom was to restrict the load hauled up the incline to 40 or 50 tons; though 18 years previous 30 tons was the limit. The train consisted of the incline brake-van, a second-class, first-class, two third-class carriages, and a brake-van.

Captain Tyler in his official report states that he found the rope very defective, and that there had been a great want of supervision over it. His previous recommendation that telegraphic communication should be established between the top and bottom of the incline had not been carried out.

The rope was tested afterwards under his supervision, and was then found adequate to bear 50% more strain than intended. There is no doubt that the rope was defective in places, it having been run over, and the damaged portion was to have been taken out on the following day. On 26th February a much stronger rope, made of copper-wire and 1¼ inches in diameter, was placed in position; telegraphic communication established between the top and bottom of the incline; and a great number of additional men set to work on the deviation line with the view of opening it by the following summer.

On the 4th of May a purse of 60 guineas, subscribed by about 300 persons, was presented to Joseph Sedman, the guard of the train, for having bravely stuck to his van during the terrible rush down the incline.

Judging from information that has recently been obtained, the origin of the accident cannot be attributed solely to the breaking of the rope, that being but one factor in the chain of events. It appears that the rope, though connected to the incline brake-van as usual, had not been hauled taut but a considerable amount of slack had been allowed to remain; further, the man whose duty it was to couple the train to the brake-van, omitted to do so. Consequently, when the train was brought up to the van, the jerk —slight as it was—started it off down the incline, the train following. When the point was reached where all the slack of the rope was taken up, the train dashed into the van, and the impetus and sudden shock naturally snapped the rope.

The incline-van had been designed by Mr. Cabry, the Loco. Supt., and was of a somewhat peculiar construction. There were no brakes whatever to the four wheels, but the whole weight of the van could be concentrated on two iron shoes that were placed just over the rails; so when considerable power was applied, the wheels were lifted from the metals, and the van simply skidded along the rails by means of the shoes.

When the guard of the incline-van applied the brake to arrest the runaway, it appears to have held for some little time, and then a shoe broke: the van, being deprived of the use of its wheels, overturned, and the carriages leapt off the line, some turning a complete somersault before coming to rest. Had the van not overturned, it is probable that all would have been well, notwithstanding the failure of the rope; for the train would most likely have kept on the line, and after reaching the level ground at the foot of the incline, Sedman would have been able to have stopped it.

On the 11th January, 1865, the *Whitby Gazette* chronicled the arrival of a train fitted with a continuous brake, and stated that three more trains, similarly equipped, were to follow. The idea was that the guard should be able to apply the brakes on several carriages by the turning of a wheel in his van, and as it is mentioned that the connection between the carriages was made by an iron bar, it is probable that the system employed was either Fay's or Newall's. These makers and others had various continuous brakes in the field then, and railway companies were testing their capabilities, but the fatal defect of most was that they were not automatic; consequently if a train broke in two, or anything went wrong with the connection, the brake was useless. Nowadays, the survival of the fittest has resulted in the elimination of all but two systems: the Automatic Vacuum Brake and the Westinghouse Air Brake. The Automatic Vacuum—vastly improved from the original Vacuum Brake, which was an extremely treacherous system—is the favourite with most companies in the British Isles. The North Eastern pinned their faith to the Westinghouse in 1878, and evidently they have seen no reason to regret the step then taken. The Vacuum is an English brake and the Westinghouse an American, both are automatic, there are slight drawbacks in each scheme, but as both give excellent results it is somewhat difficult to choose between them; personally however, the writer's preference is the Westinghouse system.

During the early part of 1865 the station at Whitby was enlarged and improved.

The Deviation line, which was originally intended to have been finished and in operation during 1864, had proved a more difficult job than anticipated, and it was not until the 1st July, 1865, that it was opened for passenger traffic. A loop at Rillington Junction had been constructed, and was brought into use on the same day, thus enabling a through service of trains to be run between Whitby and Scarboro without change of engine or carriage.

The times were as follows:

	a.m.	p.m.		a.m.	p.m.
Whitby dep.	8.0	4.45	Scarboro dep.	9.50	6.40.
Pickering ,,	8.50	5.35	Pickering ,,	10.30	7.20.
Scarboro arr.	9.30	6.15	Whitby arr.	11.20	8.10.

Mr. William Pickering was the first driver to take these trains, and it continued to be his duty for some time; he was also the driver for the experimental through trips between Scarboro and Whitby that were run three times a week before the deviation was opened.

From the local papers one gathers that excursion trains were occasionally run at very cheap fares, as seems to have been the usual practice of the North Eastern, and one which has survived to the present day. Thus on the 8th September, 1865, a return excursion left Whitby at 12 noon for York, the fares being 3s. 6d. first and 1s. 6d. covered carriages, a not excessive charge for a journey of 113 miles.

The North Yorkshire & Cleveland line had now made its way through the dales to Grosmont, where a junction was effected with the Whitby & Pickering section. This portion was opened on Monday, 2nd October, 1865, and passengers for the North were thus enabled to travel via Stockton or Middlesboro, instead of by the circuitous way of Malton and Thirsk, the only available route heretofore.

The service provided consisted of four trains each way daily between Whitby and Stockton.

Dating from the 1st January, 1870, a reduction took place in the first and second class fares throughout the whole of the North Eastern system, the first class being altered to 2d. instead of 3d. per mile and the second class to 1½d. in place of the former 2d. per mile. The alterations did not however apply to the tickets issued to the watering-places, as these fares had been revised some four years previously.

On 29th May, 1871, Maria, Marchioness of Normanby turned the first sod of the Whitby, Redcar, & Middlesborough Union Railway. The section between Saltburn and Loftus was brought into use during May 1875, and the remaining portion from Loftus to Whitby, some 16½ miles, on the 5th December, 1883.

A more direct route between Scarboro and Whitby than *via* Pickering and Rillington had long been talked about, and a company for making a railway along the coast between these towns was incorporated on 29th June, 1871. Operations were soon after commenced, but the progress of the undertaking was extremely slow. In 1876 the tunnel at Peak was completed without accident, and five years later (March 1883), the earthworks having been completed, the laying of the rails was begun. A locomotive crossed the fine red brick viaduct over the Esk for the first time on 31st October, 1884, (Fig. 23), but the line was not opened for passenger traffic until the 16th July, 1885. A few months later W. H. Hammond, Esq., J.P., of Raven Hall, Peak, died on 21st October, 1885, at the good old age of 83 ; he was an ardent promoter of the Scarborough & Whitby Railway, and was thus spared to see the accomplishment of his hopes. The line was from the first worked by the N.E.R., but in 1898 the undertaking passed entirely into their hands, and now forms an integral portion of their far-stretching system.

Parliamentary authorisation was given in 1874 to the N.E.R. bill for the construction of a railway from Pickering to the Scarborough line at Seamer Junction. Its length was about 16 miles, and its course laid through the beautiful villages of Thornton Dale, Wilton, Brompton, and Wykeham.

Negative by]   *[H. Hood, Esq.*

FIG. 22. TRAIN IN NEWTONDALE.

Negative by]   *[R. Hall, Esq.*

FIG. 23. VIADUCT CARRYING SCARBORO & WHITBY RAILWAY OVER RIVER ESK.

Like the Whitby & Loftus, North Yorkshire & Cleveland, and Scarborough & Whitby sections, the Forge Valley Line, as it is usually called, has but a single line of rails. It was opened for public traffic on 1st May, 1882, and until the Coast line was available, provided the shortest route between 'St. Hilda's Town' and the 'Brighton of the North.' Not many persons travel between these points by this line now-a-days, yet it is well worth a trial by tourists; especially those who are wise enough to make use of the facilities for cheap travel that are available to the holders of a Holiday Contract Ticket.

This practically concludes the historical portion of the present work, recent developments being considered in a subsequent chapter.

CHAPTER V.

PRESENT DAY SERVICES.

> Land of hills and woods and streams,
>   Cleveland, Cleveland !
> Fairer than a poet's dreams,
>   Cleveland, Cleveland !
> Hills with purple heather crowned,
> Woods where Autumn tints abound,
> And streams that flow with pleasant sound,
>   Cleveland, Cleveland !
>   *E. Tweddell.*

UPON carefully reviewing the railway facilities enjoyed by Whitby at the present day, there does not appear to be much cause for complaint regarding the services supplied by the North Eastern; more especially as many improvements have been made on this section of their system during the past few years. These include the acceleration of the services between London and Whitby, also of those from Stockton, Middlesboro, and the North to Whitby over the North Yorkshire & Cleveland line; the limiting of these trains somewhat to through passengers —the local traffic being provided for by running other trains either before or after the long journey services; the collection of tickets at the last stopping place; and the substitution of greatly improved rolling stock for that formerly in use, which however good in itself was not up to the standard demanded at the present day.

The chief drawbacks are slackness in the matter of punctuality —often caused, however, by events largely beyond the power of the company to control; inadequate accommodation at the stations; and at times, a general want of briskness.

As the Whitby & Pickering Railway is now a part of the North Eastern Company's system the following remarks must be taken as applying in many respects to that company generally, but in other places more particularly to the Malton, Pickering, and Whitby services. No attempt has been made to deal with the

N.E.R. as a whole : this alone would require a large volume to do justice to the subject ; moreover, it would be quite out of place in a work like this, which only treats of a small section of that gigantic system (24 miles out of a total of 1695 miles).

Analysing the train service between London (King's Cross) and Whitby, as shown in the summary tables of the N.E.R. time-books for August and December, 1905—these representing the two extremes of train accommodation—the following results are obtained.

In August there were 9 trains down (one *via* Scarboro) and the average time occupied on the journey was 6 hours 44 minutes. The best—11.30 a.m. ex King's Cross—took 6 hours, giving a journey-speed of just over 40 miles per hour. Two others, however, are not far behind, with times of 6 hours 12 minutes and 6 hours 13 minutes. The worst took 7 hours 45 minutes and ran *via* Scarboro.

Eleven trains are shown on the up journey (two *via* Scarboro), and the average time works out at 6 hours 46 minutes. Upon the whole the up service is considerably better than the down : thus there is one train performing the journey in 6 hours—curiously enough the 7.40 a.m. ex Whitby; and there are three others taking respectively 5, 8, and 9 minutes more, the last-mentioned running *via* Scarboro, and thus redeeming the poor show made by the one down train over this route. The mid-day train takes 6 hours 15 minutes, and another, *via* Scarboro, is allowed 6 hours 30 minutes. If it had not been for the unfortunate 9.0 p.m., which does not reach King's Cross till 5.50 a.m., a journey of 9 hours all but ten minutes, the average would have been far higher.

Five trains from King's Cross (one *via* Scarboro) constitute the winter service; the best taking 6 hours 51 minutes, the slowest 8 hours 6 minutes, giving an average of 7 hours 19 minutes.

The up service is again seen to be far superior to the down : out of a total of five trains, two take only 6 hours 5 minutes each, the worst 7 hours 40 minutes, while the average works out at 6 hours 51 minutes—equivalent to the time of the best down train.

Upon the whole this may be said to be a satisfactory service between London and Whitby, more especially that in force during the winter months, and one that is probably quite sufficient for the prevailing traffic.

As will be seen by the gradient table (Fig. 24), the line is an extremely hard one to work over the greater portion of its length ; and when it is considered that anything steeper than 1 in 200 tells very considerably against the speed and hauling power of the locomotive, it will cause no astonishment to find that the stretches of 1 in 48, 50, 58, 71, together with others of less inclination but still severe, reduce the speed very much and bring down the average rate of travelling considerably.

The original line was laid out on the course of a projected canal—other lines have been similarly built, and some have taken the place of canals which have been filled up to allow of the coming of their speedier rivals. Still, although the gradients of a canal may be easy, as evinced by the fewness of the locks, it does not follow that its course will be straight—it may even curve about very considerably. Here then we have the chief cause that limits the speed of the locomotive. Steep gradients may even be climbed at a high rate of speed by employing very powerful engines of suitable design, and the descending portions of the banks may be raced down at the utmost velocity which the engine is capable of acquiring, and with safety—provided that the line is straight or at any rate free from any sharp curves—but if these are present, very high speed is at once found to be out of the question. There being but little straight line in the entire 24 miles between Whitby and Pickering, and the curves being both numerous and severe, it follows that the time taken in journeying over this section will appear comparatively long, although the speed over favourable portions of the route may have been high.

Two or three seasons ago the plan was adopted of collecting the tickets of passengers at the last stopping-place before reaching Whitby. This may seem a simple idea, yet in practice it is found to greatly facilitate the working of the traffic at the terminal stations, as each train is enabled to run direct into the platforms without the stop at the ticket platform, thus economising time.

Nothing need be said here about the new rolling stock which is now employed, as it is fully described in a subsequent chapter.

Another point for commendation is the provision by the railway company of facilities calculated to remove many of the difficulties of the traveller by enabling him to find his own way about, and to obtain the information that he requires without continually bothering the station staff with questions. Such means to an end are the 'train indicators' which show the time at which a train is due to leave, the platform from which it will start, and its route and destination.

The platforms of the N.E.R. stations moreover are properly numbered; thus a so-called 'island' platform, or one with trains on each side of it, would have two numbers assigned to it, one referring to the right and the other to the left side; otherwise, if only one number be given to such a platform, the inevitable question follows: on which side is my train?

Even at the small stations a large map of the company's system is always on view, usually in the booking-hall, and available for consulting, should one wish to plan out his journey. A striking improvement, however, is the new map composed of 64 white glazed tiles, which is usually built into the wall at some prominent and easily accessible part of the station. Upon it is shown in colour the whole of the lines of the N.E. system and its connections with other companies, together with the sites of Abbeys, Cathedrals, Battlefields, &c.

Plans of the Hull, Hartlepool, Middlesboro, and Tyne Docks, all of which are owned by the Railway Company, are shown as insets. This original idea has attracted considerable attention, and its adoption has much to recommend it—being easily cleaned, very legible, practically everlasting, and permitting of correction by the insertion of a new tile or tiles as may be found necessary.

Possessing many 'beauty spots' and ideal touring districts of diverse and varied charm, the company have wisely adopted the artistic poster as a means of bringing these lovely places before the eyes of the public. A large number of these posters have been published, and a great charm is that they are produced in different styles and by various artists, thus avoiding the monotony otherwise inevitable when several views are designed and printed in exactly the same manner.

Space is not available to enumerate all, but two posters may be said to specially apply to this district, both of which I am able, through the courtesy of the company to reproduce herewith.

Fig. 15 shows an effective design of Whitby Abbey by J. F. Stackhouse, who is also responsible for the poster of Bamborough Castle, one of the first and likewise one of the most striking designs yet issued by the company. The Abbey is pourtrayed as if it had been painted upon tiles in a similar manner to the map already referred to. It is an original and uncommon idea, and attracts much attention.

The gem of the series is that entitled 'Far from the madding crowd,' a reproduction of which is employed for the frontispiece of this volume. The water-colour drawing for this poster was executed by Gordon Home. In his *Yorkshire Coast and Moorland Scenes*, there is a view taken from nearly the same spot, showing, however, by the colour scheme a slightly different time of year. Moreover the poster is treated on somewhat broader lines, as befits a picture intended for outdoor exhibition. The view point is on the old coach road at Goathland near to the bridge over the Eller Beck, and the road to Pickering may be seen climbing the hills on its way southward. In the hollow on the extreme right is Fen Bogs, the scene of much trouble in the railway's early days, and the winding chasm shows the entrance to Newton Dale, through which cañon the trains now pursue their way.

Dealing now with the failings of the line, it will not be gainsaid, I think, that many of the trains, especially during the summer months, are unpunctual to a large degree. This arises from several causes: one factor is the immense amount of luggage that is often taken by passengers, which entails the loss of much time in loading and unloading, and transferring at junctions; and which also calls for the services of a considerable number of the station staff, who thus often have to leave other important duties to attend to this matter. The average passenger, as a rule, utterly ignores the excellent arrangements that have been made by the companies for the transit of his boxes and trunks, either as Luggage in Advance or as Carted Luggage; and greatly prefers to travel having the luggage under his or her own eyes with all the attendant bother of conveyance by cab, tips to porters, labelling, claiming it at the journey's end, &c., to paying a small sum and having the whole impedimenta taken from one's house and upon arrival at destination finding it already waiting, and this without any bother whatever. The obvious remedy is to take advantage of the means provided, often at great expense, to facilitate the forwarding of luggage; and as the charges are very reasonable, there should be no excuse for passengers travelling with large quantities of luggage and inconveniencing both themselves and other people to a considerable extent. It will probably be too much to hope that these benefits will be taken advantage of to any great extent yet, nevertheless the plan of Luggage in Advance is slowly making headway amongst the public.

Another prolific cause of delay is the waiting for one or more connecting trains at junction stations. The North Eastern has many junctions upon its system—practically every few miles—and as a very large proportion of the trains are timed to connect with other trains at these points, it follows that delay to one train usually means delay to several others, simply because the connection must be made and the driver is unable or unwilling afterwards to make up the lost time. The difficulty of course is to make the connections as close as possible, yet to allow a reasonable margin for emergencies: thus if the interval between the arrival and departure of the trains at the junction is very short, a little delay in arrival on the part of one of the trains will cause the late departure of both, and in any case the time for the transference of luggage, passengers, &c., is rendered very brief. On the other hand, if ample time is allowed, passengers, especially the business section of travellers, will not fail to grumble at the long waits that have to be endured, and the journey-speed of passengers who have perforce to make two or three changes will fall to an alarmingly low figure.

The only way out of the difficulty seems to be to make the connections fairly smart, and to ensure that the porters and guards not only know their work, but what is more important, carry it out briskly.

Many of the platforms at the smaller stations are very short—adequate enough in the olden days and probably quite sufficient for the non-summer traffic of the present time, but hopelessly out of date for the lengthy trains that are employed during the season. This frequently necessitates two stops to allow of the passengers

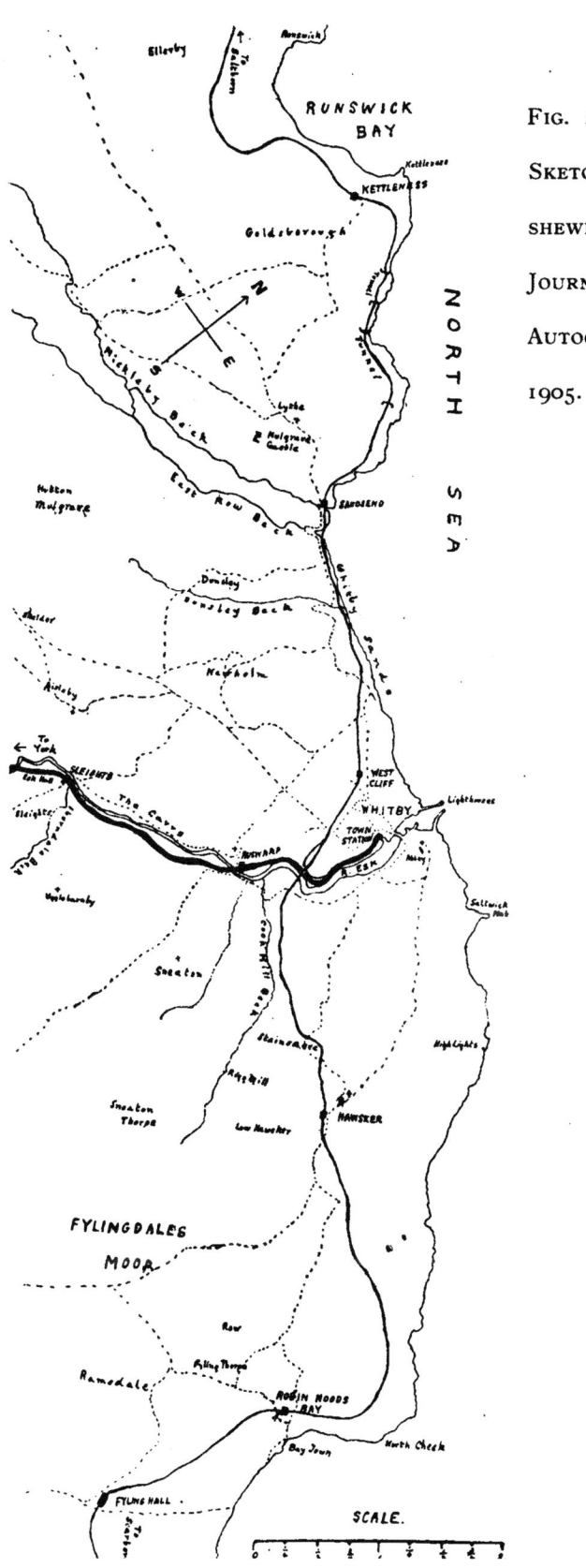

FIG. 25.
SKETCH MAP SHEWING JOURNEYS OF AUTOCAR IN 1905.

and luggage being taken in or out as the case may be; and I have known a train from Pickering to Whitby make two stops at each of the five intermediate stations for this purpose: as may be concluded, time is always lost, and is, alas, seldom regained.

To rebuild these stations or even to lengthen the platforms is, in most cases, completely out of the question, both on the score of expense and utility ; and the only way to improve matters appears to lie in a careful arrangement of the time-table, by which facilities would be provided for both the local and the through passengers. Moreover, it would seem advisable during the summer months to develop the local tourist traffic by providing a more frequent service of trains than has hitherto been the case. As there are, owing to the physical nature of the district, no other means of communication, the company has nothing to fear from competition: nevertheless, it should allow the public to participate in some of the benefits arising from a certain monopoly.

If the whole or any portions of a route are laid out as a single line only, it is evident that the liabilities to delay are greatly intensified owing to the necessity of a train having to wait at a crossing-station for the one coming in the opposite direction—notwithstanding that its own work may have been completed, and that it has been ready to proceed on its journey for some time.

Grosmont Junction is occasionally the scene of a tangle up, especially in connection with the trains running *via* Danby to Battersby, Stockton, &c. The line from Battersby to Grosmont is but a single track, and double platforms are only provided at a few of the stations. It is a matter for regret that only one platform was added to the existing two at Grosmont when the line was made, as the working thereby has been greatly hindered by the lack of accommodation for these North Yorkshire & Cleveland line trains.

To give an instance which has occurred many times: it is only necessary that the up and down Battersby trains are booked to arrive at Grosmont Junction within a short time of each other, and that the train from Battersby is late in arriving, while that from Whitby is on schedule; then there are but two courses open to the signalman at Grosmont: he can either stop the train from Whitby on the bank outside the station till the other has arrived, done its work at the station, and gone on its way; or he can allow the train from Whitby to come up to the York platform, and after arrival and departure of the other train to back out and then take up its proper route. In either case considerable inconvenience is caused to passengers, time is lost, and subsequent trains are more or less put out of their correct running.

A large amount of this unpleasantness could be obviated by the building of another platform at Grosmont to accommodate the N.Y. & C. trains : the train from Whitby could then draw up to the present platform, and there await the arrival of the other from Battersby. The running line is already there, and the necessary alterations to points, signals, and the erection of an inexpensive platform would not entail a large outlay. Moreover the present structure could, if preferred, be converted into an island platform, and the lines slewed so as to run on each side of it ; therefore I would suggest to the Directors that it is a work which should be taken in hand without delay, and that these alterations would enable the traffic over the Whitby-Grosmont section to be dealt with in a more satisfactory manner than is at present possible.

It is perhaps hardly the place to here criticise the Locomotive Department, but it certainly appears to the writer as an unbiassed observer, that time might be made up in many more cases than it usually is by smarter running on the part of the drivers, and by working the engine harder. Drivers do not like, however, to see themselves credited with a large consumption of coal, and so but little endeavour is made to regain lost time by 'extending' the engine more than usual ; the coal account therefore keeps about the average, and the driver is usually reckoned to be an economical servant to the company. A broader view of the subject should, I think, be taken by the officials ; for after safety, punctuality is surely the first thing to be studied, and if this principle be well instilled in all the company's servants, that desirable end ought to attained without very much difficulty. The saving that arises through a few pounds less of coal being burned is quickly swallowed up if time is lost and not regained, as the ill-effects of unpunctuality are far-reaching ; besides trains that are frequently late are very productive of annoyance to occasional as well as habitual travellers on the line, and these soon tend to give the company a bad name. This once acquired will prove a troublesome factor, and probably great difficulty will be experienced in getting rid of it ; even when there is little or no cause for complaint, it will be remembered, and the present good deeds of the line will not always serve as an adequate counterbalance.

The above remarks were written in the early part of 1905 before the introduction of auto-cars in the district ; however I have considered it advisable to let them remain without alteration, and to devote a few lines to the latest development of railway working.

During the summer season of 1905 the N.E.R. decided to supplement the local passenger services at certain centres by the running of steam auto-cars over various short sections of line. Scarborough and Whitby were two of the centres chosen, but the

FIG. 26. NO. 272. KITSON AND CO. 1845.

By permission of] [*J. Kitching, Esq.*

FIG. 27. NO. 494. FLETCHER'S BOGIE ENGINE AS ORIGINALLY BUILT FOR THE WHITBY BRANCH.

latter place need now only be considered. Many of the British railway companies had already built various types of rail-motors, but to Mr. Wilson Worsdell must be given the credit of designing an extremely suitable motor-carriage at a very low cost.

At the first sight the N.E.R. auto-car is apparently only an ordinary engine and carriage. Here however lies the secret of Mr. Worsdell's success: his auto-car is only an engine and carriage, but provided with special fittings to enable it to be driven from either end as may be required. Instead of purchasing new and expensive motor vehicles, or experimenting in their construction, he decided to utilise some of the old Fletcher tank engines, as modern loads and speeds are proving somewhat too much for these otherwise serviceable engines; and the results have proved very satisfactory in many ways.

When the auto-car is running with the engine in front, both driver and fireman will be on the footplate as in the usual manner; but on the return journey the fireman will remain on the engine which will now be at the rear, and the driver will take his place in the compartment at the further end of the carriage, where the necessary mechanism for controlling the engine is placed ready to his hand.

The carriage can, if required, be detached from the engine, but in the usual course of events the two will not be separated. The vehicle employed is one of the modern clerestorey bogie coaches, 52 feet in length, with five compartments for third class and one for first class passengers, thus providing seating accommodation for 58 persons. The weight of the carriage is 23¾ tons, and it will be apparent to all that there is a considerable saving in running a service like this instead of the usual train of four vehicles, equivalent to about 90 tons. Moreover, the cylinders of the engine have been reduced in size, with a view to economical working.

No time need be lost at the terminal points, for the engine has not to be placed at the other end, and the driver has simply to change his place, when all is ready for the return journey. The following table shews the daily trips worked by the Whitby auto-car in 1905; and if reference is made to the sketch map (Fig. 25), and the various changes of engine that would have been necessary in the ordinary way carefully worked out, it will give some idea as to the time saved, likewise as to the facilities given for the general working of the service.

Whitby to Robin Hood's Bay and back.
Whitby to Sleights and back.
    1 hour 40 minutes interval.

Whitby to Sleights and back.
Whitby to R.H. Bay.
R.H. Bay to West Cliff.
    1 hour interval.

West Cliff to Kettleness.
Kettleness to Whitby.
Whitby to Sleights and back.
Whitby to R.H. Bay.
R.H. Bay to West Cliff.
    30 minutes interval.
West Cliff to Kettleness.
Kettleness to Whitby.

The total mileage for one day under the above conditions is 86½ miles.

With the experience gained from the first season's working, the authorities are providing a greatly improved service during the present summer. The running of the auto-cars has been extended over many sections of the N.E.R. system, and by a re-arrangement of the time-table, and the provision of connecting trains, it is now possible to save a considerable amount of time on the journeys to and from Whitby and other large towns. The intervals between trains have in many cases been better proportioned, and the long waits at junction stations cut down. Moreover, many of the express services that in past years have not commenced until August, are this year starting in July; a great boon to those who take their holidays during that month, and especially to that class who, in largely increasing numbers, now spend a considerable portion of their time in the very pleasurable form of railway travelling. Space does not allow of full details of all the alterations, but it may be mentioned that the afternoon up train from Whitby to King's Cross is improved by 35 minutes; and that passengers by the 2.20 p.m. from King's Cross now arrive at Whitby by 8.12 p.m., a saving of 59 minutes.

CHAPTER VI.

ROLLING STOCK.

'No company has more powerful engines or better drivers; all that is wanted is stimulus.'

E. Foxwell, 1889.

ELEVEN years after the opening of the Whitby & Pickering line as a horse-railway, the first locomotive entered the town—on Friday, 4th June 1847—and from that date horse traction became a thing of the past. Few particulars are now obtainable of the engines which were first employed, the official records having long since disappeared; it has been found possible, however, to gather together one or two notes concerning some of these early locomotives.

The first engine to reach Whitby was of the four-wheeled type, the trailing pair being the drivers; or as expressed in present-day classification, 2-2-0; the first figure denoting the number of leading wheels, the second the number of driving wheels, and the third the number of trailing wheels.

The safety valves and dome were placed over the firebox. In place of the usual spokes in the driving-wheels there was substituted a solid cast-iron plate. Probably the engine bore a name, as was the almost universal custom in those days, but no record of it is now obtainable.

The driver on this notable occasion was Edward Laws and the fireman William Pickering; the former died on 23rd March 1905, after having been in the service of the company for 51 years; but the latter is still alive and in the enjoyment of excellent health.

Other early engines working to Whitby were the *Firefly* and *Greyhound*, both used for passenger traffic and of the 0-4-0 type. *Achilles* (0-6-0), a goods engine had solid driving wheels similar to that of the pioneer engine mentioned above. The boiler was lagged with strips of wood, and stirrup reversing gear was provided.

Fig. 26 represents one of the types of engine employed in the early days, and is reproduced from a photogram taken at Malton about 1872-3. No. 272 was built by Kitson in 1845, and had cylinders 13in. by 18in., and 4ft. 9in. wheels.

Other very smart looking engines of the 0-4-0 type were then also in service. These had cylinders 15ins. by 22ins., and wheels 5ft. 2in. The dome was fitted with safety valves of the Salter type. Inside frames for the engine and outside frames for the tender were adopted, the latter running upon four wheels. The number was painted on the sides of the tender, and a brass number plate was also affixed to the engine. To protect the men a weatherboard was provided. These engines were employed on both passenger and goods trains, and, although looking more like toys than machines built for real work, hauled the loads to which they were attached in an extremely satisfactory manner.

The annexed tables give such official details as are now procurable, and I am greatly indebted to Mr. Wilson Worsdell for the information contained therein, also for other matter that he has so willingly supplied, thus enabling me to make this chapter fairly complete.

No.	Maker.	Year.	Wheel Plan.	Driving Wheels.	Cylinders.
263	Stephenson	1841	2-2-2T	5' 6"	13" by 22"
264	,,	,,	0-4-0	5' 2"	15" by 22"
272	Kitson	1845	2-2-2T	4' 9"	13" by 18"
278	Murray & Jackson	1846	0-4-0	5' 2"	15" by 22"

Nos. 263 and 272 were originally single-driving six-wheeled tank engines, but were with the others rebuilt as four-coupled engines with wheels of 5ft. diameter, and cylinders 15in. by 20in.

No.	Rebuilt.	New Number.	Date.	Scrapped.
263	1859	1701	1st January, 1887	1889
264	1854	—	—	1878
272	1861	1705	1st January, 1887	1888
278	1854	1706	,,	1887

During 1864 and 1865 ten bogie engines, designed expressly for use on the Whitby branch, were built by R. Stephenson & Co., to the drawings of Mr. Edward Fletcher, the Locomotive Superintendent of the North Eastern Railway, and were numbered from 492 to 501 inclusive; the maker's numbers being 1581 to 1590. Considerable interest attaches to this class, as it was the first type of engine fitted with a bogie that had been designed by Mr. Fletcher. Fig. 27, which has been reproduced from an early photogram of these engines now in the possession of, and which has been very kindly lent to me by, Mr. John Kitching (son of Mr. Alfred Kitching of the celebrated Hopetown Foundry Works, Darlington) shows the type in its original state. It will be seen that safety valves of the spring balance or Salter type were fixed on the dome, and that a slightly raised firebox was provided. The coupled wheels were of 5ft. diameter, the bogie wheels of 3ft. diameter, and the dimensions of the cylinders were 16in. by 22in. According to the practice of those days,

Locomotive] [*Publishing Co.*
FIG. 30. No. 180 (CLASS 38), MACDONNELL.

FIG. 31. No. 472 (CLASS G1), WILSON WORSDELL.

Negative by]   *[G. W. J. Potter*

FIG. 32. NO. 65 (CLASS B.T.P.), REBUILT FLETCHER.

FIG. 33. NO. 1033 (CLASS B.T.P.), FLETCHER.

but little protection was afforded to the men, a spectacle board supported by small stays being deemed all that was necessary for provision in the way of shelter. Unfortunately the position of the print in the mount has prevented a full view of the buffers being obtained.

Fig. 28 shows the type as altered by Mr. Fletcher, and Fig. 29 is a view of the same class of engine at a later date. The latter is from a photogram by Mr. B. Mashiter, taken outside Whitby Station. Mr. G. R. Laws, the present locomotive foreman, stands on the permanent way. The driver, attired in a white jacket, is Oliver Hart, who has only recently retired from the service. He comes of a railway family, for his father and brothers have all been connected with the Whitby & Pickering line since its earliest days.

No. 1809 was originally numbered 496, but it was assigned the former number in July 1889. Upon comparing the illustrations of 494 and 1809, a few differences will be found: a lock-up safety valve is fitted on the firebox, which is larger and flush with the boiler barrel; springs have been added to the bogie, and a much larger sandbox provided; injectors take the place of pumps for feeding the boiler; and the comfort of the men has been increased by the installation of a better cab. These engines gave great satisfaction, and to the end of their career worked passenger trains between Whitby, Malton, and York; likewise over the North Yorkshire & Cleveland line to Stockton-on-Tees and West Hartlepool.

No. 500 was Mr. Pickering's engine, and retained its original boiler and firebox for over twenty years.

The following table giving dates of the re-numbering and scrapping of this class should be found useful to anyone interested in the history of North Eastern locomotives.

No.	Built.	Re-numbered.	Date.	Scrapped.
492	Sept. 1864	1807	1st July 1889	1893
493	,, ,,	1710	1st Jan. 1887	1888
494	Nov. ,,	1712	,, ,,	,,
495	Feb. 1865	1808	1st July 1889	1893
496	,, ,,	1809	,, ,,	,,
497	Mar. ,,	—	——	1883
498	Apr. ,,	—	——	1884
499	,, ,,	1713	1st Jan. 1887	1888
500	,, ,,	—	——	1884
501	May ,,	1810	1st July 1889	1893

The celebrated engine, *Brougham*, No. 164 of the Stockton & Darlington Railway, was in later years stationed for a short time at Whitby. As it was provided with a bogie and four-coupled driving wheels of only 6ft. in diameter, it would seem that the type was just what was required for the district.

In 1882 Mr. A. MacDonnell was appointed Locomotive Superintendent of the N.E.R., and the first passenger locomotives built to his drawings took the form of the graceful engines illustrated by Fig. 30. Engines of this type—officially known as Class 38—have been found to be extremely capable and speedy, moreover they are very economical in oil, coal, and repairs.

The dimensions are, driving wheels 6ft. 6in.; cylinders 17in. by 24in.; heating surface 1097 sq. ft.; and grate area 15·16 sq. ft. The weights on the bogie, driving, and trailing wheels are 12 tons 6 cwt., 14 tons 12 cwt. and 12 tons 4 cwt., respectively; giving a total of 39 tons 10 cwt. for the engine, and 66 tons 6 cwt. with the inclusion of the tender.

Some of the engines when built took the places and numbers of the earlier types that had been scrapped or renumbered, and as the tender does not wear out so rapidly as the engine, these old tenders were attached to new engines. Thus No. 38, built in 1884, has a tender over 40 years old, this being the third engine to which it has been allotted. No. 664 has the original type of tender that was designed by MacDonnell; and this engine which is stationed at Whitby, commemorates, curiously enough, the date of the synod which was held at Streonshalh (Whitby) in the year 664 to determine the correct time of celebrating Easter.

In the summer of 1894 the passenger engines stationed at Whitby, and working the Pickering, Malton, and York services, were, with the exception of a few tank locomotives, composed entirely of this class. In 1899 some new bogie carriages were introduced in place of the old four-wheeled stock, and gradually this type became general for all trains to Malton and York. Although the MacDonnell engines still did good work—No. 664 taking five of the bogie coaches up the 2½ miles of 1 in 50 and 1 in 48 from Grosmont to Goathland unaided—it was felt that with their comparatively large wheels (6ft. 6in.), and the growing weight of the trains, that the engines were approaching the limit of their powers, so the year 1903 witnessed the arrival of the G 1 class.

Twenty of these engines were built by Mr. T. W. Worsdell during 1887 and 1888, and as originally constructed were of the 2-4-0 type, and were known as class G 1. The coupled wheels were 6ft. in diameter, and the leading wheels 4ft.; the cylinders were 17in. by 24in. In 1901 No. 521, one of the class, was rebuilt by Mr. W. Worsdell with a leading bogie (4-4-0), the cylinders were enlarged to 18in., and piston valves added. The remainder have now all been similarly altered, and a very serviceable engine is the result. Among the drivers and others of the running department they are usually known as 'Waterburys'—presumably because they are good time-keepers. The comparatively small driving-wheels of the G 1 class make them suitable for hill-climbing, and enable them to get away quickly with a heavy load.

No. 472, herewith illustrated (Fig. 31) was remodelled in 1903; the view shows the engine on the new turntable at Whitby—this was brought into use in 1903, and was necessitated by the running of engines with a longer wheel-base than could be accommodated on the old table.

The 38 and G 1 classes are used chiefly on the through and fast trains during the summer months; but in the winter the working of the local passenger trains is mostly done by tank engines, three types of which may often be seen. The oldest are the Fletcher tanks with cylinders 16 or 17in. by 22in. and wheels of 5ft. in diameter. Many of these are scattered about the N.E.R. system, some differing in a few details, but the illustration of No. 1033 (Fig. 33) shows a fairly typical specimen of this useful class. The view was taken some years ago, and their present-day aspect is perhaps better represented by that of No. 65 (Fig. 32).

No. 1033 was built at Darlington in 1877, and after being once reboilered, was eventually converted at York Works in 1900 to a six-coupled side tank for shunting and train-marshalling purposes. Many others have been similarly altered, and when thus rebuilt are allotted to class No. 290; a few have also been adapted for working the steam auto-cars which were introduced at various centres last summer; Nos. 343, 585, 591, 595, 638 and others having been so treated.

Next in order come the double-ender side-tank radial engines, class A, which were first built by Mr. T. W. Worsdell in 1886. These have coupled-wheels 5ft. 6in. in diameter, and cylinders 18in. in diameter by 24in. stroke.

A very neat and pleasing design is that adopted by Mr. Wilson Worsdell for his trailing bogie side-tanks of the O class. The coupled-wheels are of the same size as those of the Fletcher tanks, namely 5ft. 0in., but the cylinders are larger and boiler pressure is higher; consequently the engines are better able to cope with heavy trains. For purposes of comparison the leading details of three types are here given. Fig. 34 shows a typical specimen of these excellent engines, and it may be remarked that to them is assigned the creditable task of hauling the heaviest loads over the difficult and exacting Coast Line between Saltburn and Scarborough.

	FLETCHER.	T. W. WORSDELL.	W. WORSDELL.
Class	B.T.P.	A	O
Wheel plan	0-4-4	2-4-2	0-4-4
Cylinders	16 × 22	18 × 24	18 × 24
Driving wheels	5′ 0″	5′ 6″	5′ 0″
Boiler pressure	140℔.	160℔.	180℔.
Grate area	17·75 sq. ft.	15·16 sq. ft.	15·16 sq. ft.
Heating surface	1074 sq. ft.	1092 sq. ft.	1097 sq. ft.
Water capacity	1000 galls.	1241 galls.	1360 galls.
Coal capacity	2 tons.	2 tons.	3 tons.
Weight when working	46 tons 3 cwt.	52 tons 6 cwt.	51 tons 9 cwt.
On leading wheels	12 t. 15 c.	L 13 t. 5 c.	L 14 t. 12 c.
On driving wheels	13 t. 8 c.	D { 11 t. 18 c. / 16 t. 6 c. }	D 15 t. 12 c.
On bogie wheels	20 t.	T 10 t. 17 c.	B 21 t. 5 c.

In contrast to the Fletcher tanks ample room for the men is provided in both the A and O classes, and side doors have been fitted to the latter with a view of minimising the unpleasant draught which is very prevalent on tank engines. The motion is much more accessible, and the convenience of the driver and fireman have been kept in view in many ways. It will not be gainsaid, I think, that upon no line have the comforts of the men been so carefully studied as upon the North Eastern in recent years. This is most decidedly as it should be; to these two men is committed the care of the train and the many lives therein, and it is only reasonable and humane to provide them with an adequate shelter, and to ensure that access to all mechanism should be made as easy as possible. Many railways still adhere to the primitive style of cab, notably the Midland; and one has only to note the engines of the various companies working into York station to see that the Great Eastern is the only line that emulates the North Eastern in size and comfort of the cab provided.

These remarks have been chiefly confined to the engines employed on passenger trains, but to those who are interested in locomotives there is a wide field for exploration to be found in the history of the numerous types of goods engines possessed by the N.E.R., and of which several varieties work into Whitby. The earlier examples, however, are gradually getting scarce since they are wearing out, and it behoves locomotive historians to be up and doing with pen and camera before the opportunity of acquiring information and pictured record is gone for ever.

No 1763, a powerful six-coupled saddle tank, shown in the view of the engine roads at Whitby (Fig. 35), used to be stationed here, and was chiefly employed in assisting the trains from Grosmont to the top of the incline by pushing in the rear. A special form of coupling was attached to the buffer beam in front actuated by a cord worked from the foot-plate, and which may be

FIG. 34. NO. 1783 (CLASS O), WILSON WORSDELL.

FIG. 35. OUTSIDE WHITBY SHEDS.

By permission of]   [*J. Kitching. Esq.*

FIG. 36. NO. 579 (CLASS 572), FLETCHER.

Negative by]   [*J. Atkinson, Whitby.*

FIG. 37. NO. 2262. SADDLE TANK ENGINE, ORIGINALLY NO. 577.

seen passing over the support that is fixed at the end of the smokebox. When the summit was reached the cord was pulled, releasing the coupling, and permitting the return of the assisting engine without the delay that would otherwise have been incurred by stopping the train to detach by hand.

Originally No. 1763 was one of a batch of twelve six-coupled goods engines numbered from 572 to 583, and built in 1866 by R. & W. Hawthorn (Maker's Nos. 1346-1357). They were designed by Mr. Fletcher, and were practically an improved edition of his 502 class of goods engine. The cylinders were 17in. by 24in., the coupled wheels 5ft. in diameter, and the boiler was fitted to blow off at 130 lbs. pressure. The block of No. 579 as shown in Fig. 36 represents the class as at first built. In 1871 No. 577 was altered to a saddle-tank engine, and fitted with wheels 4ft. in diameter, the cylinder dimensions remaining as before. Its number was changed to 1949, in January 1892, then to 1763 in January 1894, finally to 2262 in March 1899; and in 1903 it was scrapped. The accompanying photogram (Fig. 37) of the engine, bearing the number 2262, was obtained by Signalman Atkinson of Whitby, some short time before it left Whitby on its final journey.

Behind No. 1763 in Fig. 35 is No. 1602, one of the Class A tank engines, and behind that stands No. 659, a six-coupled goods engine. This was one of twenty built by R. Stephenson & Co. in 1866-7, and numbered by the N.E.R. from 642 to 661 (Maker's Nos. 1731-50). The wheels were of 5ft. diameter and cylinders 17in. by 24in. The survivors of these engines are now assigned to Class 93.

A few engines of the 1001 class may occasionally be seen here, though their numbers are now considerably less, many having been recently scrapped. They originally belonged to the Stockton & Darlington Railway, but when that company was absorbed by the North Eastern, their engines had 1000 added to their numbers in nearly all cases—hence the origin of the 1001 class.

Fig. 39 shows No. 1194, formerly No. 194 of the S. & D.R. This was designed by Mr. William Bouch, Loco. Supt. of the S. & D.R., and built by the company at their Shildon Works in 1866. The cylinders were 17in. by 24in., and wheels 4ft. 3in. in diameter. Wheel base, 11ft. 8in., divided as 6ft. 5in. and 5ft. 3in. Boiler, 4ft. 0¾in. outside diameter and 13ft. 8in. long. Heating surface of tubes, 1154 sq. ft.; firebox, 92·8 sq. ft.; total, 1246·8 sq. ft. Weight in working order, 33 tons 10 cwt., and tender about 20 tons.

The photogram was taken near Bishop Auckland about 1874, and thus represents the class in its early days, and before rebuilding had altered the original design. As will be seen by the illustration all the wheels are placed in front of the firebox, thus necessitating a much smaller space between the second and third pair of wheels than is usually allowed. The wheel base is thereby shortened, and produces a more suitable engine for traversing curves. This scheme also permits of a large firebox being employed, and ample heating surface thereby ensured. Many of these engines had the large amount of 1538·8 sq. ft. available for heating surface, distributed as to tubes, 1444 sq. ft. and fire-box, 94·8 sq. ft.

A somewhat similar type of engine, No. 1667, is shown in Fig. 38. This was built in 1860, and had wheels of 5ft. diameter, cylinders 17in. by 24in., and a tank capacity of 1450 gallons. Originally No. 1151, this was altered to 1720 in July, 1892, and to 1667 in January, 1894, and the engine was scrapped in March, 1902.

No. 958, a Fletcher tank, stands behind No. 1667, and is one of an order for twelve which were built by Neilson & Co., in 1874 (Maker's Nos. 1829-40), and numbered from 947 to 958 in the books of the N.E.R.

It is probable that some of the dimensions given in this chapter may differ from other published accounts: this may be explained by alterations occurring during rebuilding; changes in individual engines for trial purposes; and in the case of the wheels, measurements with and without tyres. However, readers may rest assured that the foregoing particulars are as correct as it is possible to make them, and that through the courtesy of Mr. W. Worsdell all the details have been officially checked.

Nothing has been said about other types of engines that may be seen at Pickering and Malton, as this would be going somewhat outside the scope of the book, moreover it would be equivalent to describing most of the many classes of engines that are possessed by the N.E.R.—a task not to be lightly undertaken.

The carriages put on by the York & North Midland Company at the conversion of the line in 1847 were of the four-wheeled type then universal. Probably they were very uncomfortable, as that company then had the unenviable reputation of providing the worst rolling stock in the kingdom for its passengers. However, with the growth of railway life improvements came; most lines adopting a larger and better type of carriage running on six wheels, some companies being far-sighted enough to introduce bogie coaches. These, as most readers are probably aware, are unequalled for smooth riding, due to the fact that the body of the carriage is supported on two bogies or trucks, each running on four wheels. As these are not attached rigidly to the framework but work on a pivot, it will readily be seen that the bogie adapts itself to the various curves encountered, consequently there is an entire absence of the unpleasant grinding and jarring usually met with when riding in four-wheeled and six-wheeled carriages.

Six-wheeled vehicles with extra play to the centre axle gradually came to be the type employed upon the Stockton and Whitby section, and five sets of these specially constructed carriages were in use in 1900; but owing to the numerous and extremely severe curves met with between Grosmont and Pickering, only four-wheeled carriages were allowed to be run between these places, and the wheel base of these was restricted to a length of 19 feet. In the view of Newtondale, shown in Fig. 22, it will be observed that the carriages are of this type, likewise that the roofs have recently been painted white. The engine hauling the train is one of those built by MacDonnell in 1884.

Certain special Great Northern four-wheeled coaches were reserved for and employed in the through service which was run to and from King's Cross during the summer months, and these were familiarly known as the 'Whitby Bathing Machines,' although they were not much worse than the average Great Northern six-wheeler. Apart from the matter of easy riding, the chief drawback of the six-wheeled vehicle is that the centre pair of wheels is invariably left brakeless; and with the high speeds of modern days, it is imperative that every wheel should be braked to insure rapid deceleration of speed.

The standard of rolling-stock provided by the N.E.R. has been steadily rising within the last few years, and in the summer of 1899 it was decided, with a view of bringing the Whitby and Malton services more up-to-date, to try some specially built bogie coaches over this section. The running proved very satisfactory, and as the vehicles passed over the curves easily and safely, this type was adopted in place of the four-wheelers hitherto standard on this portion of the system.

The new coaches are no less than 45ft. in length, and from the official photogram reproduced in Fig. 40, it will be seen that clerestory roofs are fitted; and although non-corridor, access to a lavatory can be obtained from certain compartments. Both third and first class divisions are finely upholstered and lit with gas, ample space being allowed for the occupants. Artistic photographs of some of the many beautiful places in the territory of the N.E.R. are placed in each compartment.

The weight ranges from $20\frac{1}{2}$ tons to $23\frac{1}{4}$ tons; but there should be no difficulty in ascertaining the correct weight of any particular coach, as this is painted on the framework under the footboards at one end of the carriage; a practice that might be adopted with advantage by other companies.

Several of the curves have recently been made less severe, thus improving the travelling; and now in place of the old four-wheelers hitherto compulsory, it is the practice to run bogie coaches of 45, 49, and 52ft. in length.

To conclude this chapter a diagram is given, (Fig. 41) wherein is depicted an early colliery engine built by Stephenson, and in contrast, Worsdell's latest six-coupled giant; the roofed, but open-sided, carriage of 1838, and the luxurious twelve-wheeled dining car of the East Coast Joint Stock—otherwise the Great Northern, North Eastern, and North British Railways; together with the evolution of the huge 40 ton bogie mineral truck from the primitive chaldron wagon. For leave to reproduce this interesting plan I am indebted to the late Mr. J. R. Fletcher, M. Inst., C.E., who had the original prepared in 1901 to illustrate his paper on 'The Development of the Railway System in Northumberland and Durham.'

Locomotive] [*Publishing Co.*
FIG. 38. NOS. 1667, 958, AND 664.

FIG. 39. NO. 1194 (CLASS 1001), BOUCH.

FIG. 40. BOGIE COACH, 45FT.

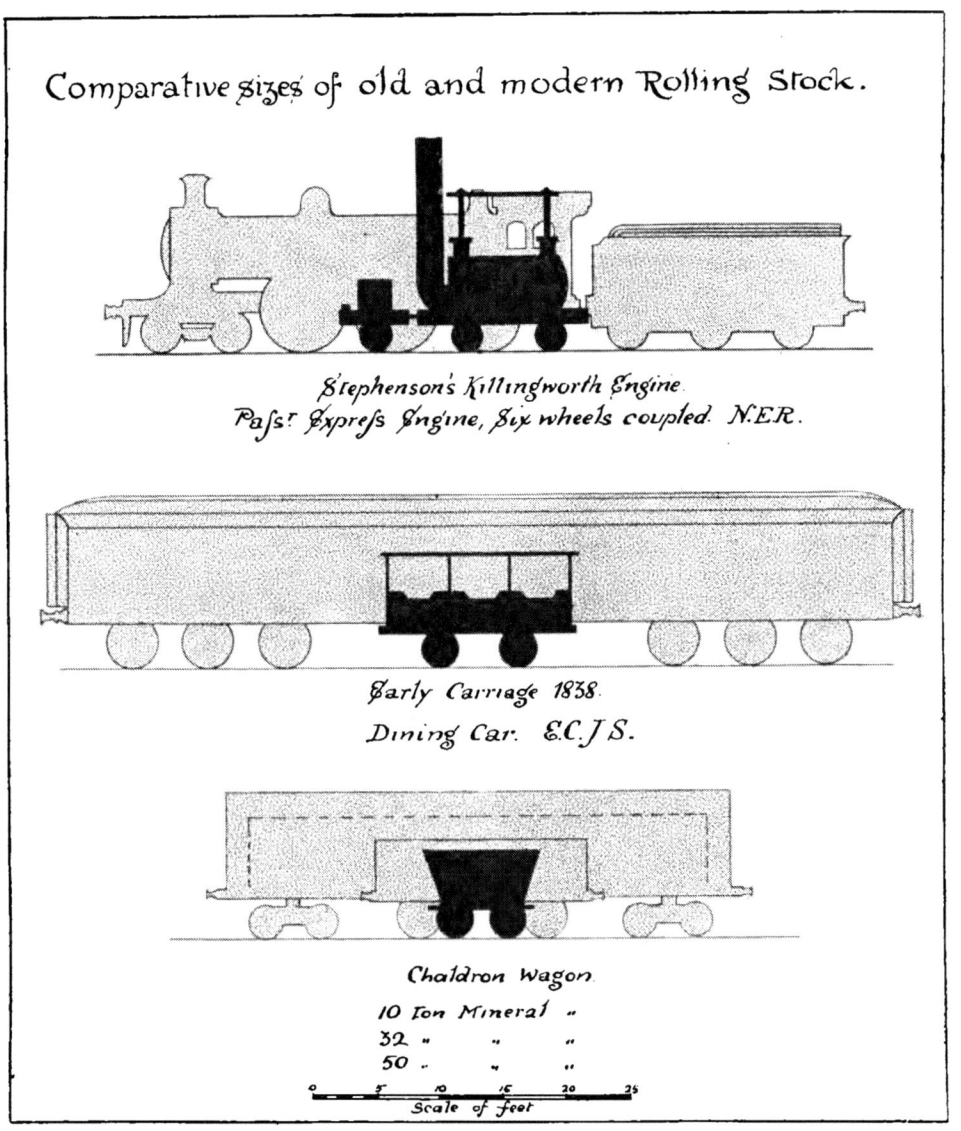

Comparative sizes of old and modern Rolling Stock.

Stephenson's Killingworth Engine.
Pass.^r Express Engine, Six wheels coupled. N.E.R.

Early Carriage 1838.
Dining Car. E.C.J.S.

Chaldron Wagon.
10 Ton Mineral "
32 " " "
50 " " "

Scale of feet

By permission of]   [J. R. Fletcher, Esq.

FIG. 41. ROLLING STOCK DIAGRAM.

CHAPTER VII.

A JOURNEY OVER THE W. & P.R.

'It is difficult to suppose a more pleasing and romantic route than through the woody gill, shaded by lofty cliffs, crowned with rugged rocks, which, under the names of Pickering Dale, Newton Dale, and Godeland Dale, conduct us to the picturesque Vale of Esk and Port of Whitby.'

Professor Phillips.

PERHAPS it is hardly necessary to say that the initials W. & P.R. stand for the 'Whitby & Pickering Railway,' but at least two other and not inappropriate meanings may be deduced therefrom: the 'Winding and Picturesque Railway,' a title that the line certainly deserves; and the 'Wild and Primitive Railway,' a designation belonging more especially to its early days. A further conceit may be propounded: the 'White and Purple Route'—in autumn, when the heather is in full bloom there would be no difficulty in proving the fitness of the latter epithet; and in spring, the masses of flower on the many hawthorn trees, and the wild roses, white and pink, would certainly justify the former part of the phrase.

There are few railway rides in England at all like this, and at whatever season the traveller may select for his journey there are always beautiful sights to be gazed upon; and those to whom a love of nature has been granted will revel in the many varied and gorgeous effects of sky and land here so bountifully displayed.

Leaving the substantial stone-built station of Pickering with its roof of white and purple glass, its garden gay with flowers, and the grass-grown remains of the Castle towering above, the line takes its way through fairly open country, the Pickering Beck keeping close to the track. It will be seen that trees have been planted on the slopes leading up to the Castle walls, various winding walks made, and a number of seats provided for the convenience of visitors and inhabitants of the town.

From the commencement to the end of the journey the line is seldom far away from running-water, and of a truth it may be said by the traveller that the becks—like the poor—are always with us; beck being the usual term in this district for these moorland streams, and equivalent to the brook of the south-country man. The insignificant little beck and the magnificent cañon through which we are to pass seem very disproportionate, and lead to the conclusion that other agencies than this small stream have formed this long, winding, and imposing valley. Judging from an excellent article by Professor P. F. Kendall, it seems most probable that Newton Dale was formed by the overflow from a huge lake that was situated in Eskdale during the Glacial period, and calculated by him to have been about 11 miles long and not less than 400 feet deep.

Soon the ground begins to rise on each side, and large plantations of firs, pines, and ash trees stretch down to the railway, making an extremely pleasant prospect. As the valley winds, so the line follows its course, frequently necessitating some very sharp curves; but in the standard bogie stock no inconvenience is felt, and the smooth running of these vehicles is a great improvement on that of the old four-wheeled carriages.

Little by little the genial aspect of the country vanishes, the heather makes its appearance, trees get scarcer, and the scenery sterner and grander; few houses are seen, and these are either small farmsteads or the houses of platelayers and other railway servants. About four miles from Pickering, near a disused quarry and railway siding on the left, a valley with the usual beck in the centre may be seen on the right: this leads to Lockton and Levisham, but the villages are not visible from the line. After a run of another two miles Levisham station is reached, a quaint little spot seemingly removed from nearly all habitation. The Pickering Beck—which has been for some considerable distance on the left—soon crosses to the right of the track, directly afterwards returning to its previous side: in this short loop will be seen on the west or left hand what was originally Raindale Inn. This is the place at which the horses were kept in the early days of the line; the stables may still be seen at the back of the house, which is now a private residence and known as 'The Grange.'

Up to this point the gradients have been very easy but now the real climbing commences, and stretches of 1 in 86, 58, and 50 are encountered. Soon afterwards a glimpse may be caught of Raindale Mill, a quaint old-fashioned building with its wooden overshot wheel, where Raindale with its attendant beck runs into Newton Dale from the west. Following the bend of the line around Skelton Tower, a building placed high on the cliff at the right hand side, some disused iron works are seen on the same cliff a little distance along. It is most interesting, and rather a novel experience, to sit by the window and watch the engine going round some sharp curve in front. Several times upon looking out no visible opening can be seen, but just at the last the track veers suddenly to one side, and another section or meander of the line, comes into view.

Professor Kendall has well described the characteristic scenic features in the following words:—'In each meander of one of these valleys the outer curve is steep, sometimes precipitous, while the inner curve has a more gentle slope. These features are nowhere more beautifully displayed than in the upper portion of Newton Dale above Raindale Mill. Here, for several miles, the railway from Pickering to Whitby runs through a superb cañon having a depth of 300 or 400 feet, and occupied through a part of the distance by a small stream, the Pickering Beck. The outsides of the meanders here are in many cases so precipitous as to be unscalable.'

The Newton Dale signal cabin is at length passed, the engine puffing slowly and sonorously, while the line still winds and climbs among the bracken, heather, and hawthorn bushes; plenty of moorland streams and boggy places abounding on each side, and forming veritable traps for the unwary pedestrian.

Another curve is rounded, the beck recrossed, and Killingnoble Scar, a fine semi-circular range of rock, is seen on the north or left hand side—the railway here running for a short time almost due east. These cliffs have been noted for considerably over 200 years as the breeding-place of a celebrated strain of hawks, and it is only quite recently that the birds have become extinct. At the end of this meander is Needle Point, a large rock crowning the angular extremity of the cliff, and having a clearly visible perforation, thus often called the Needle's Eye.

North Dale is next entered, and after another two miles of climbing, Fen Bogs, the spot that caused so much trouble to the original constructors of the line, is reached. From here is obtained a fine view of the moors in all their spacious solemnity, stretching away on all sides; beautiful in spring, they are still more so in autumn, when in a different harmony of colour, they take on the most lovely tints and shades of purple, green, and brown. No signs of life are apparent, except that there may possibly come into view a few wild moorland sheep, white and black, usually with horns, and as nimble as goats. The high road—in more than one sense—from Whitby to Pickering, here runs parallel to the railway for a short distance, and a glimpse of it may be caught as it makes its way in the distance up the hill side.

Summit Cabin, situated at an altitude of 550 feet, is soon reached, and shortly after the deviation line is entered upon, the course of the old railway being noted by a bridge on the left close to some stone buildings known as Goathland Gate Houses. At this point the road to Goathland from the Pickering road runs in from the moors on the right, crossing the Eller Beck by a low stone bridge.

The country now regains its original cheerfulness, and cottages appear with gardens full of old-time flowers and stately holly hocks.

Goathland, 8½ miles from Levisham, the last station, is situated amidst delightful scenery, and is increasingly the resort of visitors from all parts. The old water-mill, not now in use however, may be seen close to the railway, hence the original name of the station—Goathland Mill. Fig. 20 will give an idea of the station and its surroundings. Whinstone is here quarried from the cliff, and part of the works may be seen on the right. The station itself is on a slope of 1 in 105, and the gradient then changes to 1 in 50 and soon after to 1 in 48, so when the brakes are released the train moves gently out of the station and rapidly gathers speed, necessitating frequent applications of the Westinghouse brake.

A charming view of Darn Holm, a prettily situated house is obtained on the right, then after passing through a deep cutting, the line suddenly curves round and a most delightful prospect of the country far below is obtained, together with pleasant glimpses of Beck Hole and the course of the original line. Here the track runs, as it were, on the very edge of the cliffs with a sheer drop of 100 feet. This height, however, is rapidly reduced, and soon the old route is joined near the Deviation Junction signal cabin. A short tunnel is passed through, the Murk Esk crossed and the station of Grosmont reached.

The illustration of Grosmont station (Fig. 19) is taken from the down platform, looking back in the direction of Pickering. Deviation Junction cabin is visible through the tunnel, and a pillar of the original tunnel may just be discerned to the left of the more modern erection. By turning to Fig. 18, a view is obtained through the tunnel from the other end; the building there seen is the Grosmont cabin which is situated at the end of the down platform. The North Yorkshire & Cleveland branch from Picton Junction and Middlesboro, by way of Battersby and Castleton, here joins the Whitby and Pickering section.

Grosmont—locally Growmond—was once a pretty little village in a hollow surrounded by hills, but ironstone was discovered, furnaces were soon built and in operation, and huge heaps of slag arose to disfigure the surroundings. The furnaces have long since been closed, but still the tall chimney, ruined buildings, and slag heaps remain, a melancholy memorial of departed prosperity. However, it is possible that Grosmont may resume activity as a mining centre, for at the time of writing, (June 1906), negotiations are taking place, it is stated, with a view to the purchase and re-opening of the mines in this locality. The better quality of the iron ore found in the Middlesboro district caused the abandonment of the Grosmont industry; but the presumed approaching exhaustion of the former, coupled with improved modern means of smelting, &c., has induced the ironmasters to again look upon Grosmont with a favourable eye.

Hence the remainder of the journey to Whitby lies close by the banks of the Esk, which is crossed and recrossed several times within the next three miles. Soon the new red-tiled church of Aislaby may be seen high up on the hills at the left hand, and the white stone church and long stretched-out village of Sleights on the right. At the top of the village and by the edge of the moor is the steep and dangerous Blue Bank, and it was by this route that the coaches from Pickering used to make their way into Whitby, descending the village street and crossing the railway by the station, thence by the level Carrs to Ruswarp, where another hill had to be climbed and another descent faced before their journey was ended. The cluster of houses near Sleights station form the little hamlet of Briggswath.

Fig. 21 is a photogram of Sleights station, looking up the line, and gives a fairly good idea of the well-wooded and picturesque scenery that is characteristic of this part of Yorkshire.

The Esk is navigable for small pleasure boats as far as Sleights Bridge, it being dammed up at Ruswarp for the purpose of working the large corn mill situated there. During the summer months this part of the river is usually gay with merry boating parties. The river is crossed for the last time just before reaching Ruswarp station, where tickets are collected from all trains which stop there. Soon after resuming the journey the line runs under the huge red brick viaduct (Fig. 23) carrying the Scarborough & Whitby Railway over the deep valley of the Esk, and the loop from the West Cliff station, descending sharply on the left, joins the Pickering line at Bog Hall. Directly afterwards the train glides slowly into the curved station of Whitby, the 'Winding and Picturesque Railway' maintaining its character to the last, and the journey to the 'Haven under the Hill' is accomplished.

THE END.

INDEX.

Entries in *Italics* refer to books, papers, etc.

'A.B'	6
Accidents	37, 49, 50, 52—54
'Achilles'	67
Act of Parliament	17, 39, 42, 46, 47, 52
'A Looker on'	20
Alum	6, 9, 22
Amalgamation	41, 46, 50, 56
'Amicus'	3
Analysis of Train Services	59
Arrowsmith, A. & J.	35
Athenaeum	35, 36
Autocar	64—66, 71
Beck Hole	15, 24, 27, 80
Belcher, H.	25, 31, 39, 40
Black Bull	43, 44
Blue Bank	5, 15, 81
Boghall	20, 81
Bolckow, Vaughan, & Co.	36
Bouch, W.	73
Bradshaw	35, 40, 41, 44, 45
Brakes	29, 53, 54, 75, 80
Bridges	18, 21, 23, 50
Briggswath	81
Brocka Beck	15, 16
Brock Hole Beck	15, 16
Brodrick	21
'Brougham'	70
Cab	72
Cabry	54
Campion, R.	5, 7, 9, 16, 20, 26, 38
Canal	1, 4, 5, 60
Cañon	61
Carriages	29, 74—76
'C.D.'	6
Chapman, Aaron	16, 44
,, Abel	37
,, T.	51
Cholmley, Col. G.	6
Clark, T.	31
Coal	6, 8, 10, 12, 36, 64
Coast Line	5, 52, 56, 57, 71
Conservatives	16, 38, 51
Construction	20
Crosley	4

Curves	26, 60, 75
Cuttings	22
Descriptions, Geological	15
Deviation Line	51, 52, 54, 55, 80, 81
Directors	18
Distances	26, 34
Disused Line	80
Diversion of Esk	17, 21
Dodgson, G. H.	31, 32
Drivers	43, 62, 64, 65
Easter	70
Edge-rail-way	18
Edinburgh & Dalkeith Railway	29
Elections	16, 44, 51, 52
Eller Beck	4, 24, 61, 79
Elliot, Sir G.	44
Engines	19, 42, 64, 65, 67—74
Esk	1, 4—10, 13, 17, 21, 23, 37
Esk Dale Lake	78
Estimates	7, 12—14, 16, 20
Evolution of an English Town	32, 33
Excursions	48, 51, 55
Fares	19, 41, 42, 45, 50, 52, 56
Fay	55
Fen Bogs	24, 25, 50, 61, 79
'Firefly'	67
Fishburn, T.	26, 41
Flags	27
Fletcher, E.	65, 68, 69, 71—74
,, J. R.	76
Forge Valley	57
Gauge	17, 25
Goathland	24, 79, 80
Goods Engines	67, 72—74
Gradients	5, 6, 8, 13, 15, 16, 24, 26, 59
Great Eastern Railway	72
Great Northern Railway	75
'Greyhound'	67
Grosmont	23, 63, 70, 81
Hammond, W. H.	56
Handbook for Railway Travellers	33
Harding	27
Hart, O.	69
Helmsley	5, 10, 31
High Marishes	43, 44
Holiday Annual	35
Home, G.	32, 61
Horse traction	8, 29, 30, 33, 47, 48, 67
Hudson, G.	41, 44, 51
Hugill, J.	6
Incline	13, 15, 19, 24, 27, 29, 30, 37, 51—54, 72

Incline Van ...	54
Iron Stone ...	9, 24, 36, 47, 80, 81
Jeans, J. S. ...	2
Jessop, W. ...	18
Journey Speed ...	59, 62
Jubilee of Railway System ...	2
Junctions ...	62
Kendall, P. F. ...	78, 79
Killingnoble Scar. ...	79
King's Cross...	59
Kirby ...	43—45
Kirby Moorside ...	5, 10
Kitching, J. ...	68
Knox, R. ...	15, 16
'Lady Hilda'...	28, 30
Laws, E. ...	67
—— G. R. ...	69
Lawyers ...	19
Leeds ...	10, 41
Leeds & Thirsk Railway ...	47
Leeds Northern Railway ...	46, 47
Levisham ...	78
Liberals ...	38, 51
Liverpool ...	6, 32, 41
Liverpool & Manchester Railway ...	6, 25
Loftus ...	56, 57
London & North Western Railway ...	32
Loop, Rillington ...	55
Low Marishes ...	43
Luggage ...	42, 61
Macdonnell, A, ...	70, 75
Malton ...	1, 3, 5, 6, 10, 12, 20, 52, 56, 69, 70
Maps ...	34, 35, 39, 60, 65
Marishes ...	44
Meetings ...	7, 9, 16, 41, 50
Middlesboro' ...	11, 36, 41, 56, 58, 61, 81
Midland Railway ...	15, 72
Mogg, E. ...	35
Moorsom, R. ...	16
Murk Esk ...	23, 50, 80
Needle's Eye ...	79
Newall ...	55
Newton Dale...	4, 24, 25, 32, 33, 37, 61, 75, 78, 79
North Eastern Railway ...	46, 50
—— Failings of ...	61—64
—— Lines purchased by ...	50, 56
—— Travelling facilities ...	58—61
North Yorkshire & Cleveland Railway	47, 51, 52, 56, 57, 63, 64, 80
Openings ...	3, 26, 42, 43, 52, 56, 57
Outram, B. ...	18

iv.

Passenger Duty	42, 43
Pickering	1, 3—6, 10—14, 16, 18, 20, 26, 28, 30—32, 77
—— Beck	17, 25, 77—79
—— W.	53, 55, 67
Picture of Whitby	40
Plate-way	18
Platforms	60, 62—64
Posters	61
Postillion	29, 30
'Premier'	30
Punctuality	61—65
Quickest trains	59
Radclyffe, E.	32
Rails	14, 17, 18, 25
Rainbow	33
Raindale Inn	26, 30, 78
—— Mill	30, 78, 79
Remarks in favour	47
Reports	7, 10, 16, 39—41
Rillington	42, 43, 49, 52, 55
Rope	53, 54
'Royal Mail'	1
Ruswarp	5, 21, 81
Sale of Line	15, 16, 41
Saltburn & Whitby Railway	71
Scarbro'	1, 3, 5, 15, 31, 37, 41, 42, 44, 48, 49, 51, 52, 55, 71
Scarbro' & Whitby Railway	5, 31, 56, 57, 71, 81
Scenery of W. & P.R.	31
Sedman, J.	43, 53
Shares	2, 16, 17, 38, 39
Shipbuilding	6, 20, 43
Signals	44
Single line	63
Sleepers	18, 25
Sleights	5, 20—23, 81
Snow	37
Speed limitations	60
Stage coach	1, 30, 31, 43
Stations	17, 21, 43, 44, 52, 55
Stephenson, G.	10, 32, 36, 39, 76
—— R.	44, 51
Stockton	1, 5, 7, 56, 58, 69, 74
Stockton & Darlington Railway	2, 3, 7, 8, 10, 11, 41, 70, 73
Stokesley	7, 8
Stone blocks	14, 18, 25
Storey, T.	7—11
Streonshalh	70
Subscription list	2, 9, 16
Summit cabin	79
Survey	9, 11, 79
Swanwick	27

Thompson, H. S.	50, 51
———— W.	20, 47
Thoughts on a Railway	10
Time Table	40, 41, 44, 45, 48, 49, 55
Tolls	19
'Townsman, A'	10
Traffic returns	36
Train service	30, 59
'Transit'	30
Trucks	29
Tunnel	23, 80
———— Inn	26, 27, 40
Turnbull, W.	30
Turnpike road	1, 3, 5
Turntable	71
Turton, E.	17
Vacuum Brake	55
Viaduct	56, 81
Wagons	29
Walker	35
Wardell, W.	29, 30
'Waterburys'	71
Weighing Machine House	21
Westinghouse Brake	55, 80
Whinstone	12, 20, 23, 80
Whishaw, F.	25, 29
Whitby Abbey	61
W. & Grosmont Lime Company	27, 36
W. & P.R.; An Impartial Examination	20
———— *its probable traffic*	20
'Whitby Bathing Machines'	75
Whitby Borough	16
Whitby Gazette	48, 50—52, 54
Whitby Repository	3, 6
Whitby Stone Company	21, 23, 27, 36
Woodford	37
Worsdell, T. W.	70, 71
———— W.	65, 68, 70, 71, 74, 76
York	1, 10, 40, 44, 48, 50, 55, 69—72
York & North Midland Railway	16, 30, 41, 42, 46, 74
York, Newcastle & Berwick Railway	46
Yorkshire Coast and Moorland Scenes	61
Young, Dr. G.	40

CPSIA information can be obtained at www.ICGtesting.com
Printed in the USA
LVOW091925061112

306129LV00016B/3/P